Collaborative Models for Clinical Practice

Collaborative Models for Clinical Practice

Reflections from the Field

Edited by Philip E. Bernhardt,
Thomas R. Conway,
and Greer M. Richardson

ROWMAN & LITTLEFIELD
Lanham • Boulder • New York • London

Published by Rowman & Littlefield
An imprint of The Rowman & Littlefield Publishing Group, Inc.
4501 Forbes Boulevard, Suite 200, Lanham, Maryland 20706
www.rowman.com

6 Tinworth Street, London SE11 5AL, United Kingdom

Copyright © 2021 by Philip E. Bernhardt, Thomas R. Conway, and Greer Richardson

All rights reserved. No part of this book may be reproduced in any form or by any electronic or mechanical means, including information storage and retrieval systems, without written permission from the publisher, except by a reviewer who may quote passages in a review.

British Library Cataloguing in Publication Information Available

Library of Congress Cataloging-in-Publication Data
Library of Congress Cataloging-in-Publication Data
Names: Bernhardt, Philip E., 1977– editor. | Conway, Thomas R., 1972– editor. | Richardson, Greer, 1967– editor.
Title: Collaborative models for clinical practice : reflections from the field / edited by Philip E. Bernhardt, Ed. D., Thomas Conway, Ed. D., and Greer Richardson, Ph.D.
Description: Lanham : Rowman & Littlefield Publishers, 2020. | Includes bibliographical references.
Identifiers: LCCN 2020033337 (print) | LCCN 2020033338 (ebook) | ISBN 9781475858143 (Cloth : acid-free paper) | ISBN 9781475858150 (Paperback : acid-free paper) | ISBN 9781475858167 (ePub)
Subjects: LCSH: Teachers—Training of. | Mentoring in education.
Classification: LCC LB1707 .C645 2020 (print) | LCC LB1707 (ebook) | DDC 370.71/1—dc23
LC record available at https://lccn.loc.gov/2020033337
LC ebook record available at https://lccn.loc.gov/2020033338

Contents

Foreword   vii

Acknowledgments   xi

Introduction   xiii

1   Valuing the Expertise of School-Based Teacher Educators in School-University Partnerships : Creating a Sustainable Model of Mentor-Teacher Preparation   1
Kristien Zenkov, PhD; Audra Parker, PhD; and Holly Glaser, MAT

2   The Teacher Educators and Mentors (TEAM) Model: A Full-Year Clinical Residency Program   15
*Amy Vessel, EdD, and Dawn Basinger, EdD,
Louisiana Tech University*

3   A Model for Success: A Modified Yearlong Clinical Internship   33
*Amy M. Rogers, PhD, and Courtney A. Dexter, PhD,
Lycoming College*

4   Building Relationships and Resilience in a Teacher Residency Program: Strategies for Successful Clinical Experiences   47
*John Lando Carter, EdD; Josh Tipton, EdD; and
Ashlee Hover, EdD; Middle Tennessee State University*

5   Empowering All Voices: Meaningful Mentoring Designed
    for a University-School Partnership   59
    Christopher Clinton, EdD, and Maureen P. Hall, PhD,
    University of Massachusetts Dartmouth

6   Mentoring the Mentors: Developing Culturally Efficacious
    Educators within a Residency Model   73
    Jennifer Gilardi Swoyer, PhD; Lorena Claeys, PhD;
    Belinda Bustos Flores, PhD; Claudia Treviño García, PhD;
    Lucinda Juárez, PhD; Lisa Santillán, PhD; Lucinda N. Sohn, PhD;
    The University of Texas at San Antonio

7   The Identification, Selection, and Evaluation of Mentor-
    Teachers within a Professional Development School Setting   85
    Timothy Lintner, PhD; Bridget Coleman, PhD; Jeremy Rinder, MS;
    Deborah McMurtrie, PhD; University of South Carolina Aiken

8   Partners in Learning: Building Mentoring Partnerships through
    a Shared Learning Experience   97
    Rachelle Curcio, PhD, University of South Carolina;
    Alyson Adams, PhD, University of Florida

9   Realizing Inspiring and Successful Educators (RISE):
    A University-School District Partnership to Support Latinx
    Teacher-Candidates   109
    Sheri Hardee, PhD, and Lauren Johnson, PhD,
    University of North Georgia

10 Searching for Partnerships to Transform Clinical Practice
    Experiences: A Case Study   127
    Blake West, EdD, National Education Association

About the Editors   139
About the Contributors   141

Foreword

In 2018–2019, I was fortunate to be elected president of the Association of Teacher Educators. The vision and theme of my presidency focused on clinical practice within the context of preparing our future teachers. Part of the opportunity I was given in this leadership role was to form a task force that would carry on the theme of my conference. Thus, the Task Force on Addressing the Needs of Cooperating/Mentor/Associate Teachers in Their Practices and Roles as Mentors and Supervisors of the Novice Teacher was launched with appointments of co-chairs Dr. Philip E. Bernhardt, Dr. Thomas R. Conway, and Dr. Greer M. Richardson.

This book is one of the key initiatives of this task force. In this foreword, I explain the catalyst for the book and the background for this initiative that in some ways is nothing short of serendipitous, but it also has strong grounding in the influence and impact of the ATE professional community. As a career-long teacher educator, I have advocated for attending to the needs of the school-based teacher educator and adjunct supervisor. They are the forgotten group in the funding equations of policymakers who do not consider the value of supporting and resourcing the professional development needs of a teacher educator. How did I evolve this passion?

As a doctoral student, I was fortunate to be situated as a graduate assistant in the Office of Laboratory Experiences at the University of Maryland, College Park. There I assisted the director, Dr. James Greenberg, in managing the five teacher education centers that were part of the mutually funded teacher preparation partnerships with the area school systems.

Coming into doctoral studies as a former elementary teacher, my world expanded into teacher education, and there a new identity and passion was formed. I was mentored by a cadre of stellar teacher center coordinators and my director, who consistently engaged in inquiry about their practices, shared their research, and modeled new pedagogies associated with their practices. They were practitioner-scholars before the term was popular as it is today.

My doctoral studies led me to understand in deeper ways the many dilemmas and ethical issues associated with the teacher educator's boundary-spanning roles, and how the needs of the cooperating/mentor teacher needed to be addressed in equal proportion to the teacher-candidate. Upon finishing my doctorate, I went on to George Washington University, assuming the role of director of the GWU Office of Laboratory Experiences.

There I continued to develop, with colleagues, a course in supervision and mentoring for our doctoral students, who were the ones often assigned to cover field supervision in our teacher-preparation programs. One of my students was Philip Bernhardt, who took the reins in advocating for better resources and professional development for the cooperating/mentor teacher. His inquiry for my course involved developing an academy for cooperating/mentor teachers with his peer—Dr. Vince O'Neill; and later as he moved into academe, he continued this work at the Metropolitan State University of Denver.

We have remained connected through ATE, and now with the opportunity to create a task force, Philip was my first choice in exploring how we could put this initiative together. Dr. Bernhardt was already well on the way to developing the vision for this book, which became integrated into the task force initiative, and which pulled in more like-minded colleagues in Tom Conway and Greer Richardson —all stellar practitioner-scholars in teacher education.

I have observed a consistent theme in policy reports and standards on teacher preparation (AACTE, 2018; AACTE, 2010; AASCU, 2017; ATE, 2018; ATE, 2016; CAEP, 2018; CCSSO, 2012; Flessner & Lecklider, 2018; NCATE, 2010) that call for renewed emphasis on the clinical practice components of teacher-preparation programs that need stronger connections between theory and practice as well as attention to teacher educator pedagogical practices (i.e., *approximations of practice*—Grossman, 2010) that provide mediated opportunities for the novice teacher to apply their knowledge, skills, and dispositions toward their professional roles in real school contexts.

ATE has a longstanding history in: developing the preservice field-experience standards and teacher educator standards (ATE, 2018; ATE, 2016), and attracting and developing programs and initiatives focused on supporting the teacher-educator's work and scholarship (i.e., ATE Clinical Fellows Symposium, 2020). In fact, ATE was originally founded in 1920 as the National Association of Directors of Supervised Student Teaching (Flessner & Lecklider, 2017).

Foreword

As ATE's scope and reach has expanded to encompass both school- and university-based professionals who prepare and develop teachers, limited attention has been paid to the needs of the cooperating/mentor/associate teacher. In particular, attention is needed in preparing them to effectively enact their essential roles in supervision and mentoring.

It is most gratifying to see an ATE scholarly product dedicated to addressing the needs of the school-based cooperating/mentor teacher and the adjunct university supervisor. These individuals play an essential role in teacher preparation and ensure the growth and development of our future teachers. However, in many programs' designs they are loosely connected to the faculty who teach the curriculum.

The work they do constitutes the intangibles, including the unexplained recurring phenomena attributed to bridging the complexities associated with: (a) different personalities and orientations toward teaching practice; (b) mediating the different situations that arise between needs of teacher-candidates and cooperating/mentor-teachers to ensure a continued productive partnership; (c) and, most importantly, negotiating productive experiences for all the participants involved.

Through critical conversations of objective observational data aligned to frameworks for effective teaching, teacher educators navigate, negotiate, mentor, direct, coach, assess, and evaluate; and they provide many types of resources and emotional support as needed for teacher-candidate growth. The role of the teacher educator in the clinical realm of teacher preparation represents nuanced practices that can make or break the motivational state of a pre-service teacher; and it can impact their successful completion of requirements for teacher licensure.

This publication provides a window into the practices that sit in the "third space" (Cuenca, Schmeichel, Butler, Dinkelman, & Nichols, 2011) of teacher preparation; and the foundational relationship-building processes that lead to trust and the establishment of productive relationships for those involved.

I applaud the teacher educator practitioner-scholars who have contributed to this work. They are the new leaders in this line of inquiry. My hope is that the reader will find inspiration, ideas, and models to build on in their own contexts, as well as new knowledge and understandings that will assist them in their continuous improvement efforts associated with exemplary clinical preparation of pre-service teachers.

Patricia Sari Tate, PhD
George Washington University
ATE president 2018–2019

REFERENCES

American Association of State Colleges and Universities Teacher Preparation (2018). *A pivot toward clinical practice, its lexicon, and the renewal of education preparation: A report of the AACTE Clinical Practice Commission.* Washington, DC: Author.

American Association of State Colleges and Universities *Teacher Preparation Task Force (2017). Preparing teachers in today's challenging context: Key issues, policy directions, and implications for leaders of AASCU universities.* Washington, DC: Author.

Association of Teacher Educators (2020). 2020 clinical practice fellow symposium. Manassas, VA: Author. Retrieved from https://ate1.org/clinical-practice-fellow and https://ate1.org/cpf_video.

Association of Teacher Educators (2018). *ATE Standards for teacher educators.* Manassas, VA: Author.

Association of Teacher Educators (2016). *ATE Standards for field experiences in teacher education.* Manassas, VA: Author.

Council for Accreditation of Teacher Preparation Programs (2019). *CAEP handbook: Initial level programs.* Washington, DC Author.

Council of Chief State School Officers (2012). *Our responsibility, our promise: Transforming educator preparation and entry into the profession.* Washington, DC: Author.

Cuenca, A., Schmeichel, M., Butler, B., Dinkelman, T., & Nichols, J. R. (2011). Creating a "third space" in student teaching: Implications for the university supervisor's status as outsider. *Teaching and Teacher Education, 27*, 1068–77.

Flessner, R., & Lecklider, D. R. (Eds.). (2017). *The power of clinical preparation in teacher education.* Rowman & Littlefield: New York.

Grossman, P. (2010). Learning to practice: The design of clinical experiences in teacher preparation. *Policy brief: Partnership for teacher quality.* Washington, DC: National Education Association.

National Council for the Accreditation of Teacher Education (2010). *Transforming teacher education through clinical practice: A national strategy to prepare effective teachers.* Washington, DC: Author.

Acknowledgments

We would like to fondly thank Patricia Sari Tate, PhD, past president (2018–2019) of the Association of Teacher Educators (ATE) for supporting, encouraging, and helping to vision this edited text. Pat also invited us to lead an ATE task force focusing on supporting the needs of mentor-teacher and university-based educators; the text is a product of this work. Dr. Tate is a leader in the field, and this book is a tribute to her tireless work to influence and advance teacher preparation in meaningful and significant ways. We are thankful for her guidance, kindness, and gracious wisdom.

We would also like to acknowledge a number of individuals who supported this project as guest editors. As experts in mentoring and clinical experiences, each of these individuals contributed powerful insights across the various chapters. A special note of gratitude goes to Thomas Sutton, Amy Rogers, Karen Dunlap, Patricia Tate, Rubén Garza, Romena Holbert, Vince O'Neill, and Sheila Conway.

This text is a compilation of ten unique projects representing a diverse set of teacher-preparation programs. Each chapter tells a story of transformation, development, and renewal. We want to thank all the authors for the work they are currently engaged in to improve mentoring practices, clinical experiences, and the overall educational experiences for their teacher-candidates. Providing a forum for teacher educators to share their stories has been a tremendous learning experience, and we feel grateful for this opportunity. We hope you find the projects both instructive and inspiring as you consider how to enhance and develop your own preparation program.

Finally, we want to acknowledge that projects such as these are only possible through the support and encouragement of our families. A huge thank-you to Ellen, Emma, and Oliver Bernhardt, Brian and Parker Wilson, and Thoth Weeda for supporting each of us as we spent time putting this text together.

Introduction

In recent years, the National Council for Accreditation of Teacher Education (NCATE, 2010), the Association of Teacher Educators (ATE, 2016), and the American Association of College for Teacher Education (AACTE, 2018) have each called for teacher preparation programs to situate clinical practice at the center of curricula. As part of this work, there is an emphasis on developing intentional, mutually beneficial partnerships between educator preparation programs, schools, and districts to support clinical practice. Within these partnership endeavors, there is a critical need to better prepare those professionals tasked with supporting teacher-candidates during their clinical experiences. While there is certainly guidance in the literature highlighting instructive approaches for developing effective partnerships as well as preparing and supporting mentor-teachers and university-based educators, there is tremendous value in listening to and learning from preparation programs that are systematically and successfully engaged in this work and positively impacting teacher-candidates.

There is clear consensus within the field that clinical practice, supported by well-prepared and supported mentor-teachers and university-based educators, is critical for the successful preparation of teacher-candidates (AACTE, 2013, 2018; Clarke et al., 2014; Darling-Hammond, 2000; NCATE, 2010). Whether candidates are enrolled in a traditional undergraduate or graduate preparation program, a residency-based pathway, or are seeking one of the numerous alternative routes to licensure, it is essential to match them with experienced and prepared professionals who understand how to support their cognitive, emotional, and pedagogical development.

This thoughtful pairing is essential as teacher-candidates tend to view their field-based experiences as the most significant component of the preparation process and perceive their mentor-teachers as essential to their success (Clarke et al., 2014; Kirk et al., 2006; Weiss & Weiss, 2001). Nonetheless, within many educator programs, the current practices for preparing mentor-teachers and university-based educators to be effective clinical coaches is often inadequate and fails to fully address their roles, responsibilities, and expectations (Clarke et al., 2014). Unfortunately, this highly impactful element of the educator preparation process just does not typically garner the time, focus, or necessary resources that it deserves.

There is an extensive body of research supporting the assertion that mentor-teachers and university-based educators who are professionally prepared with the requisite skills, knowledge, understandings, and dispositions are a cornerstone of clinical practice (AACTE, 2018; Grossman et al., 2009; Flessner & Lecklder, 2017a; 2017b; Darling-Hammond, 2014; Hammerness et al., 2005; Hollins, 2015). That said, many preparation programs lack systematic approaches and strategies for preparing mentors and university-based educators for the important task of coaching, supervising, and evaluating teacher-candidates during the clinical portions of their program (Aspfors & Fransson, 2015; Izadinia, 2015; Sayeski & Paulsen, 2012; Smith & Avetisian, 2011). As a result, these practitioners do not always receive the necessary development and support to be effective in their role.

In the publication *A Pivot Toward Clinical Practice, Its Lexicon, and the Renewal of Educator Preparation*, the AACTE Clinical Practice Commission (2018) offered ten proclamations for effective clinical practice. In particular, the mutual benefit proclamation posits that school-based and university-based educators are essential to the success of teacher-candidates as they "play necessary, vital and synergistic roles in clinical preparation programs" (p. 33). When writing the chapters included in this text, authors were asked to consider two primary questions connected to this proclamation to help them develop and shape their narratives highlighting partnerships and collaborative endeavors.

1. How do teacher preparation programs develop mentor-teachers and university-based educators as effective clinical coaches?
2. How do teacher preparation programs work in collaboration with schools to support teacher-candidates during clinical internship?

The primary purpose of the chapters included in this edited text are to provide readers a varied set of examples from teacher preparation programs that have established effective systems, practices, and pedagogies to develop and support mentor-teachers and university-based educators in becoming effective clinical coaches. The text endeavors to shine a bright light on those programmatic efforts shaping teacher preparation in impactful, meaningful, and sustainable ways. This text will be of primary interest to all those working in organizations, institutes of higher education, alternative licensure programs, schools, and districts involved with the preparation of teacher-candidates.

As you read through the chapters in this book, we asked the authors to use AACTE's Clinical Practice Commission's *Lexicon of Practice* (2018) to provide consistency with terminology. They are included here for your reference:

1. *Clinical practice:* Teacher-candidates work in partnered educational settings engaged in teaching that is closely integrated into coursework.
2. *Clinical coaching:* The practices in which school and university teacher educators engage including supervision and mentoring.
3. *Clinical internship:* The clinical experience in which the teacher-candidates assume full responsibility for pedagogy and are mentored/coached by school and university teacher educators.
4. *Mentor-teacher:* The school-based teacher educator paired with the teacher-candidate.
5. *Teacher-candidate:* Those enrolled in teacher preparation programs.
6. *Teacher-preparation*: The work done to prepare teacher-candidates for entry into the profession.
7. *School-based teacher educator:* Assumes responsibilities for mentoring and partnership and has the school as his or her institutional home.
8. *University-based teacher educator:* Assumes responsibilities of evaluation, coaching and instruction, and partnership and has the university as his or her institutional home.

REFERENCES

American Association Colleges of Teacher Education (2013). *The clinical preparation of teachers: A policy brief.* Washington, DC: Author.

American Association for Colleges of Teacher Education. (2018). *A pivot toward clinical practice, its lexicon, and the renewal of educator preparation: A report of the AACTE clinical practice commission.* Retrieved from https://secure.aacte.org/apps/rl/res_get.php?fid=3750&ref=rl.

Aspfors, J., & Fransson, G. (2015). Research on mentor education for mentors of newly qualified teachers: A qualitative meta-synthesis. *Teaching and Teacher Education, 48,* 75–86.

Association of Teacher Educators (2016). *Standards for Field Experiences in Teacher Education*. Fairfax, VA: Author.

Clarke, A., Triggs,V., & Nielsen, W. (2014). CTs participation in teacher education: A review of the literature. *Review of Educational Research, 84*(2), 162–202.

Darling-Hammond, L. (2000). How teacher education matters. *Journal of Teacher Education, 51*(3), 166–73.

Darling-Hammond, L. (2014). Strengthening clinical preparation: The Holy Grail of teacher Education. *Peabody Journal of Education, 89*(4), 547–61.

Flessner, R., & Lecklder, D. (2017a). *The power of clinical preparation in teacher education: Embedding teacher preparation within P–12 school contexts*. Lanham, MD: Rowman & Littlefield.

Flessner, R, & Lecklder, D. (2017b). *Case studies of clinical preparation in teacher education: An examination of three teacher preparation partnerships*. Lanham, MD: Rowman & Littlefield.

Grossman, P., Hammerness, K., & McDonald, M. (2009). Redefining teaching, reimagining teacher education. *Teachers and Teaching: Theory and Practice, 15*(2), 273–89.

Hammerness, K., Darling-Hammond, L., Grossman, P., Rust, F., & Shulman, L. (2005). The design of teacher education programs. In L. Darling-Hammond & J. Bransford (Eds.), *Preparing teachers for a changing world: What teachers should learn and be able to do* (pp. 390–441). San Francisco, CA: Jossey-Bass.

Hollins, E. R. (2015). *Rethinking field experiences in preservice teacher preparation: Meeting new challenges for accountability*. New York: Routledge.

Izadinia, M. (2015). A closer look at the role of mentor teachers in shaping preservice teachers' professional identity. *Teaching and Teacher Education, 52*, 1–10.

Kirk, D., Macdonald, D., & O'Sullivan, M. (2006). *The handbook of physical education*. London: Sage.

National Council for the Accreditation of Teacher Education. (2010). *Transforming teacher education through clinical practice: A national strategy to prepare effective teachers*. Washington, DC: Author.

Sayeski, K. L., & Paulsen, K. J. (2012). Student teacher evaluations of cooperating teachers as indices of effective mentoring. *Teacher Education Quarterly, 39*(2), 117–30.

Smith, E. R., & Avetisian, V. (2011). Learning to teach with two mentors: Revisiting the "two-worlds pitfall" in student teaching. *The Teacher Educator, 46*(4), 335–54.

Weiss, E. M., & Weiss, S. (2001). Doing reflective supervision with student teachers in a professional development school culture. *Reflective Practice, 2*, 125–54.

Chapter One

Valuing the Expertise of School-Based Teacher Educators in School-University Partnerships

Creating a Sustainable Model of Mentor-Teacher Preparation

Kristien Zenkov, PhD; Audra Parker, PhD; and Holly Glaser, MAT

Answering recent calls from scholarly and policy reports, professional associations, and accreditation agencies, educator preparation is in the midst of a national shift toward clinically centered teacher preparation (AACTE, 2018; CAEP, 2014; Zeichner, 2013). Informed by the conclusions of the NCATE Blue Ribbon Panel Report, *Transforming Teacher Education through Clinical Practice: A National Strategy to Prepare Effective Teachers* (2010), this teacher education preparation paradigm centers efforts in school-based contexts—rather than in university settings—while merging teacher-candidates' prospects for professional applications of pedagogical skills with their academic learning.

The importance of these theory/practice connections have recently been revisited in the white paper *A Pivot Toward Clinical Practice, Its Lexicon, and the Renewal of Educator Preparation* (AACTE, 2018). It is within this context that mentor-teachers—who serve as the primary school-based teacher-educators for candidates in their culminating clinical experiences—are gaining increased attention (Hobson, Ashby, Malderez & Tomlinson, 2009).

As the key link between learning theory and the application of pedagogical strategies, mentor-teachers are understood by university-based teacher-educators to be "experts of practice" (Butler & Cuenca, 2012, p. 297). As well, teacher-candidates frequently identify their internships and mentor-teachers as the most important factors in their professional preparation (Valencia, Martin, Place, & Grossman, 2012).

Yet the roles of mentor-teachers and their preparation for such essential capacities are largely unexamined (Childre & Van Rie, 2015; Hudson & Hudson, 2010; Ulvik & Sunde, 2013). Mentors are often chosen in a haphazard way (Russell & Russell, 2011) and are seldom provided substantive training to guide future teachers (Butler & Cuenca, 2012). This manuscript outlines efforts to respond to these traditions and assumptions via a sustainable approach to training PK–12 mentor-teachers to serve as boundary-spanning, school-based teacher educators.

Recognizing that a curriculum for mentor-teachers should be realized in partnership with the experts who routinely serve in these school-based teacher educator roles, over the past two years the authors have collaborated with the subjects of this training in the design and implementation of two rounds of instructional efforts. An overview of the scholarship on mentor-teachers and their training is provided, then a description of the mentor training modules, followed by consideration of module implementation. The chapter closes with a discussion of the implications of these mentor training efforts for the field of educator preparation.

LITERATURE REVIEW

The release of the NCATE Blue Ribbon Panel Report in 2010 represented a pivot for the field of teacher education and its associated literature (NCATE, 2010). The report called for educator preparation programs to place clinical practice at the center of their endeavors, turning teacher education "upside down" (AASCU, 2017; CAEP, 2014; Zenkov, Parker, Parsons, Pellegrino, & Pytash, 2017).

This pivot was rooted in the traditions of the Professional Development School (PDS) model, and it aimed to highlight the role of boundary-spanning university and school-based teacher educators (ATE, 2015; Fisher & Many, 2014; Holmes Group, 2007; Ipkeze, Broikou, Hildenbrand, & Gladstone-Brown, 2012; NAPDS, 2008; Parker, Zenkov, & Dennis, 2019).

This swing has also resulted in reforms from numerous teacher education professional associations, including the requirement of the Council for Accreditation of Educator Preparation (CAEP) and the Association for Advancing Quality in Educator Preparation (AAQEP)—echoed by the recommendations of AACTE's "Clinical Practice Commission" (CPC)—that educator preparation programs expand the role that school-based personnel play in teacher education efforts (AACTE, 2018; AAQEP, 2019; CAEP, 2013).

The primary theoretical origin of the mentor training structures that have been developed are shaped by the notion of "third space." This concept has its basis in hybridity theory (Soja, 1996), which suggests that individuals draw on multiple discourses and cultures to make sense of given contexts (Rochielle & Carpenter, 2015; Rutherford, 1990). This theory also highlights the fact that being "in between" multiple points of view—for example, university-based teacher educators, classroom teachers and mentor-teachers, teacher-candidates, and even PK–12 students operating between university and school perspectives—can be simultaneously constructive and constraining (Feiman-Nemser, 1998; Zenkov & Pytash, 2018).

The concept of "third space" promotes a critical pedagogical orientation to teacher education ventures (Martin, Snow, & Franklin Torrez, 2011; Williams, 2014). This concept explicitly intends to bridge the culture of PK–12 schools—with their emphasis on the everyday aspects and outcomes of teaching—and the culture of the university—with its focus on research and theory (Cuenca, Schmeichel, Butler, Dinkelman, & Nichols, 2011).

Unfortunately, many of the studies of "third space" structures suggest that these are not sustainable, too often maintain the disconnect between coursework and classroom practice, and fail to thoroughly consider the positionality of players who are attempting to move between university and school contexts (Lavadenz & Hollins, 2015; Sawyer, Neel, & Coulter, 2016; Zeichner & Bier, 2015). By contrast, the mentor training model described here explicitly aims to address these detachment and sustainability critiques (Anthony, Averill, & Drake, 2018; Richmond, Bartell, & Floden, 2017).

Mentoring—or the act of guiding a teacher-candidate's individualized professional development (Norman & Feiman-Nemser, 2005) through a combination of "showing and telling, asking and listening" (van Ginkel, Verloop, & Denessen, 2016, p. 1010)—is a complicated activity (Feiman-Nemser, 2001). Beliefs about mentoring are shaped by prior experiences in being mentored into the profession and daily work with colleagues (Cochran-Smith & Paris, 1995; Hall, Draper, Smith & Bullough, 2008).

Scholars have conceived of numerous mentoring models, most often through a consideration of the roles that mentors serve, including as parent figures, troubleshooters, counselors, supporters, and instructional guides (Boreen, Johnson, Niday, & Potts, 2000; Richter et al., 2013). Butler and Cuenca (2012) detailed how mentors serve in three roles—as emotional support systems, instructional coaches, and socializing agents.

Schatz-Oppenheimer (2017) suggested five categories of effective mentoring traits: spheres of professional responsibility, knowledge of teaching and mentoring processes, personality characteristics, professional skills associated with mentoring, and evaluation. Hall and colleagues (2008) surveyed 264 mentor-teachers to determine how mentors understood their functions, suggesting mentors viewed their roles in one of four ways, with most (73 percent) describing their work as providing professional and emotional support to novice teachers.

Van Ginkel and colleagues (2016) have recently suggested that the literature on mentoring echoes Orland-Barak and Klein's (2005) findings that there seem to be two discrete conceptions: "instrumental" notions, concerned with providing candidates effective teaching fundamentals, and "developmental" notions, rooted in collaborative reflections between the teacher-candidate and mentor. Most mentors continue to conceptualize their work as "cooperating teachers" rather than as guides involved in co-teaching (Hall et al., 2008, p. 343).

Much less has been written about the means of preparing effective mentors. As research has shown, simply having experience as a teacher and a mentor should not be conflated with actual mentor training (Ulvik & Sunde, 2013), and the delivery of mentor instruction can vary in time, mode, and nature (Childre & Van Rie, 2015; Russell & Russell, 2011).

Diverse topics are addressed in such trainings—from communicating program requirements to developing evidence-based teaching practices. Delivery might occur solely through face-to-face seminars, online modules, or a hybrid of both. Hudson and Hudson (2010) recommend including opportunities for new mentors to shadow experienced mentors as an essential component of such trainings. Hobson and colleagues (2009) suggest mentor-teacher preparation efforts should be oriented toward developing skills indicative of highly effective mentors, including attention to strategies for working with adult learners, engaging in feedback cycles, and scaffolding reflection on teaching and learning.

In addition, given the enduring nature of previous experiences, mentor training should also support mentors' personal professional development (Hobson et al., 2009). As well, inquiry oriented-mentoring is one model that aims to serve as an effective professional development tool for mentor-teachers (Yendol-Hoppey, Dana, & Delane, 2009). Ultimately, a primary factor in mentor training is time to discuss mentoring experiences at regular intervals with colleagues (Hobson et al., 2009; Hudson & Hudson, 2010; Hudson, 2013).

A decade ago, Hobson et al. (2009) suggested studies of effective mentor training should be a "priority area" for future research—an opinion since echoed by other teacher education researchers (Childre & Van Rie, 2015; Ulvik & Sunde, 2013). Scholars have identified other factors that play a role in the success of mentor training, including dedicated time provided by schools for mentoring—though the provision of time is rarely under the control of trainings' designers, who are typically university faculty members.

Russell and Russell (2011) answered Hobson et al.'s call and explored U.S. secondary school mentor-teachers' conceptions of mentoring and development of mentoring skills through a two-day, face-to-face workshop model.

Ulvik and Sunde (2013) examined a yearlong hybrid training program for secondary mentors in Norway consisting of eight face-to-face workshops and online components. Participants shared through questionnaires and focus groups that they gained mentoring knowledge and skills through the training, but thought this training was most effective for those who already had mentoring experience.

As these and other studies demonstrate, the evidence base for effective mentoring programs remains uneven and thin. Research reports are typically focused on particular contexts, lack rich descriptions, and most often reflect a "top-down" approach to training. In response to these limited examinations and Hobson and colleagues' (2009) recommendation, for the program discussed in this chapter the primary goal was to co-create a replicable, sustainable, widely applicable mentor training curriculum that reduced the disconnect between school and university contexts. And by examining two rounds of the implementation of this model, it is hoped the chapter contributes to the evidence base on mentor training outcomes.

CREATING A MODEL FOR MENTOR-TEACHER TRAINING

Supported by grants from the Virginia Department of Education, the authors have implemented and examined two iterations of a mentor training program in a large public university context with four licensure programs—elementary education and secondary education programs in the first year, then integrating special education and physical education programs the second year. The elementary education program had a twenty-plus-year history of employing a PDS framework with its educator preparation efforts and currently works with twenty-eight school partners.

The secondary education (SEED) program more recently adopted a PDS orientation and has grown to include seventeen partner schools. The special education and physical education programs operated with a traditional placement model for teacher-candidates, but had shifted their structures to partner with intentionally selected schools and mentor-teachers, supported by university faculty and school liaison roles.

Mentors in all teacher-preparation programs partnering with the college of education had access to online mentor training modules but were not required to complete these. The five online modules, designed in response to national accreditation requirements, took approximately ten hours to complete and addressed a broad range of topics applicable to all preparation programs in the college, including key organizational structures in the college, common internship tasks, and general guidelines for mentoring teacher-candidates.

While the modules contained important foundational information for new mentors, they did not address the skills identified in the research literature as critical for effective mentoring of teacher-candidates.

YEAR ONE MODULES AND RESEARCH METHODS

In the first year of the grant-supported "Advanced Mentor Training" project, a series of five face-to-face modules for elementary and secondary mentor-teachers were designed and implemented. These were intended to address the instructional gaps that the research literature highlighted. The authors worked with partner school administrators to identify thirty-two exceptional mentors from across partnerships to serve as participants, with the goals that 1) they would provide critical feedback as they participated in each module and 2) following participation, they would lead subsequent iterations of their training in their school sites or area clusters. Each mentor received a $1,500 honorarium for their involvement in the pilot implementation and module revision efforts.

Module 1 provided a context for mentoring efforts and focused on co-constructing an understanding of the attributes of effective mentors and mentoring. This included discussion of how mentors might scaffold their mentees' transitions into their classrooms, their consideration of shared (though not equal) teaching roles, and reflections on effective mentoring practices and roles in contexts other than education. Module 1 culminated in a multi-session development of a mentoring readiness tool that is now central to many of the programs' mentor selection activities.

Module 2 formally introduced co-planning and co-teaching as essential activities for supporting a gradual shift in responsibilities from mentor to teacher-candidate. Six models of co-teaching ("one teach, one assist," "alternative teaching," "station teaching," "one teach, one observe," "parallel teaching," and "teaming") are described, and it is discussed how the structures of the settings—elementary and secondary schools—supported and restricted the implementation of these models. Participants were also asked to follow up on this session by documenting (via video recording) examples of co-teaching in their own classroom/school contexts.

While it was anticipated that an equal amount of time would be spent with each of these five modules, participants were particularly interested in the notions/practices of mentor readiness/selection and models of co-teaching; these topics received additional attention in the third project session. As a result—and with time further abbreviated as the result of multiple snow days—Modules 3, 4, and 5 were compressed into the two final sessions.

Module 3 required mentors to explore their own experiences with giving and receiving feedback and various formats of feedback methods (e.g., in person vs. video coding). In Module 4, mentors engaged in activities related to having difficult conversations about pedagogical practices with teacher-candidates and their teaching peers. Module 5 served as a summative session to a shared inquiry, focusing on mentor-teachers' ongoing professional development and consideration of overall revisions to future iterations of the training.

Given the limits of space and interest in also sharing the evolution of these trainings for the second-year of implementation, here analysis methods and findings for these Year 1 activities are briefly detailed (Parker, Zenkov, & Glaser, 2019). Data collected included module artifacts, participant and instructor reflections, and midpoint and end of training surveys. Content and thematic analysis guided consideration of these data (Patton, 2002; Saldana, 2016).

Through iterative rounds of qualitative analysis, three themes were identified: (1) what mentors told us about mentoring, (2) mentors' roles in clinical practice, and (3) the quality, relevance, and impact of the training. Here, just the findings related to the nature of the training are discussed, as these were the primary insights considered to revise and implement a second-year version of the training.

Analyses revealed the modules addressing co-planning/co-teaching, giving feedback, and challenging conversations were most relevant to mentors' needs and interests (Parker, Zenkov, & Glaser, 2019). Mentors indicated that they developed a greater understanding of how to apply co-teaching models to working with teacher-candidates as a result of the training. Similarly, mentors described an increased confidence in providing targeted feedback to teacher-candidates and in navigating difficult conversations.

Specifically, they acknowledged that the training supported their abilities to provide clear, direct, and even difficult feedback that was purposeful in its delivery and timing. Lastly, participation in the modules facilitated mentors' growth through reflection and reengagement with the fundamentals of their teaching practices. While it was intended to have Year 1 participants implement this training in their own school sites, it was clear at the conclusion of this pilot that further revisions to the modules were necessary before such an expectation was reasonable.

YEAR TWO REVISIONS AND INITIAL FINDINGS

A review of the findings from Year 1 informed the significant revisions made to Year 2 grant-supported implementation. While in Year 1 mentors had experienced the content of each module and shared their perspectives on the content, evaluation of the program revealed an over-reliance on the five-module structure, that mentor-teachers' expertise was not sufficiently honored, and differentiated needs of the elementary and secondary mentors were not fully considered.

For Year 2, there was a continued focus on designing a sustainable approach to this training; however, it was recognized that it must be explicitly responsive to each of the involved programs. To do this, small teams of highly effective mentors (two to six per program) and one university-based teacher educator were identified from each of four programs (elementary, secondary, special education, physical education).

In Year 2, instead of spreading the training across the entire school year, the authors met with participants for three early summer days to consider what advanced mentor training should look like for each of the various programs. Focusing on one module at a time, brief overviews of each module's objectives and sample activities, readings, videos, and field-based application activities were shared. The bulk of each two-to-three-hour morning or afternoon session was then spent with mentor training participants—trainers-in-training—considering their specific programs and fields, colleagues, contexts, and own mentoring experiences as they designed the revised versions of each module for the anticipated fall 2019 training implementation for each of their programs.

While only initial data collection and program evaluations of the Year 2 implementation has been completed, preliminary analyses of post-training survey data from these Year 2 participants revealed key themes related to the nature, content, format, and application of the training modules. These mentor "trainers-in-training" consistently noted that the project itself was "empowering."

They highlighted how they were treated in a uniquely respectful manner as compared with most professional development opportunities they had previously experienced, and how they had already developed authentic relationships with other educators (peers from other schools and university faculty). They were clear that they were crafting meaningful curricula that incorporated flexibility in content that would allow these to be relevant to their respective subject areas, grade levels, and school sites.

The primary "takeaways" of Year 2 implementation were related to the themes of professional respect, positioning (Bullough & Draper, 2004), and stance. Participants shared and demonstrated—in the form of their profound engagement and their detailed revisions to module curricula—that because they were being honored with a deeper level of professional respect as school-based teacher educators they were willing to "own" the development of the mentor training curricula and the implementation of these materials in ways that we did not anticipate and could not have called for.

The authors now understand that such trainings must be differentiated by licensure program—and perhaps by program site—and that university-based teacher educators must continue to position school-based teacher educators as what they are: the experts on both mentoring practices and mentor training. Likewise, we must shift our stances as university-based teacher educators, using language and engaging in collaborative structures that clearly reflect a willingness to yield pedagogical control to school-based partners.

Across respondents from four distinct licensure areas, they expressed an interest in knowing more about their specific program requirements and course sequences. They also posed questions about the next steps—asking about opportunities to practice their newly developed training presentations and about how they would be able to follow up with the new mentors with whom they would implement these pilot training structures. Notably, while it had clearly not been reasonable for Year 1 participants to implement what in retrospect impressed us as a generic training content, the authors are confident that Year 2 participants will share their abbreviated, responsive curricula with their program- and school-specific colleagues in the coming months.

IMPLICATIONS

For those of us who have been involved with educator preparation for at least a decade, it seems useful to consider a weather or climate change analogy to describe the current state of the field: teacher education is facing a crisis akin to a once-every-100-year storm, with seismic shifts in our nation's confidence in the effectiveness of educator preparation structures and traditional, university-based teacher educators (NCATE, 2010; Schneider, 2018).

The authors of this chapter, who represent a continuum and range of teacher education experiences, grade levels, and subject areas—largely view this predicament as an opportunity to suggest and study vastly different organizational elements than those encountered in our own teacher preparation and that we have enacted as teacher educators. The primary promise of the current reforms in the educator preparation field is in practitioners', policy makers', and scholars' recognition that it is essential to learn to *live* the value of "school-based teacher educators" and to honor their expertise through their involvement in all teacher education endeavors.

The two iterations of advanced mentor training reported in this chapter represent a dynamic approach to the creation and implementation of professional development for school-based teacher educators; in fact, the dynamism of these trainings is likely best represented by the very explicit ways that these evolved from professional development *for* mentors to professional development *by* and *with* these mentor experts.

As the first implementation of the mentor training was reviewed, the authors were impressed by the still significant work needed to help school-based teacher educators see themselves in this new way. The design and outcomes of the second version of this training have highlighted that what is lost in the uniformity of training structures might be gained in program-specific quality and relevance.

This identity shift and participants' difficulty in making the transition from teacher and mentor to one individual in their own classroom, to "advanced" mentor-teacher who would be responsible for the development of the coaching skills of their professional peers, was one of the most significant themes of final surveys completed by participants after Year 1 of the program. As a result, concerted effort was made to cede pedagogical power to the Year 2 participants.

While the research-based objectives for the advanced mentor training piloted in Year 1 were provided, Year 2 participants were provided with tremendous latitude to determine how these objectives would be met—with their "people," in their subject areas, in their schools. It can be asserted that this might have been the primary task of university-based teacher educators: offering these future mentor trainers the agency that comes with having knowledge of such research-based parameters. And it is believed that this agency facilitated Year 2 participants' creation of training content and modes that addressed their field-specific needs.

This work with exceptional mentors across two implementation cycles repeatedly and demonstrably highlighted the untapped expertise of these school-based teacher educators. As university-based teacher educators, we bring a specialized knowledge and honed skill sets to teacher preparation efforts. However, the authors are increasingly confident that clinical teacher preparation activities would evolve more quickly and effectively if more time was spent on building its foundations by developing school-based teacher-educators as equal partners in this work.

REFERENCES

American Association of Colleges for Teacher Education. (2018). *A pivot toward clinical practices, its lexicon, and the renewal of educator preparation: A report of the AACTE Clinical Practice Commission.* Washington, DC: Author.

American Association of State Colleges and Universities Teacher Preparation Task Force (AASCU). (2017). *Preparing teachers in today's challenging context: Key issues, policy directions, and implications for leaders of AASCU universities.* Washington, DC: Author. Retrieved from https://www.aascu.org/AcademicAffairs/TeacherEdReport.pdf.

Anthony, G. & Averill, R., & Drake, M. (2018). Occasioning teacher-educators' learning through practice-based teacher education. *Mathematics Teacher Education and Development, 20*(3), 4–19.

Association for Advancing Quality in Educator Preparation (AAQEP). (2019). *A guide to AAQEP accreditation.* Fairfax Station, Virginia: Author.

Association of Teacher Educators (2015). *Revised standards for field experience.*

Boreen, J., Johnson, M.K., Niday, D., & Potts, J. (2000). Mentoring beginning teachers. York, ME: Stenhouse.

Bullough, R. V., & Draper, R. J. (2004). Making sense of a failed triad: Mentors, university supervisors, and positioning theory. *Journal of Teacher Education, 55*(5), 407–20.

Butler, B. M., & Cuenca, A. (2012). Conceptualizing the roles of mentor teachers during student teaching. *Action in Teacher Education, 34*(4), 296–308.

Childre, A. L., & Van Rie, G. L. (2015). Mentor teacher training: A hybrid model to promote partnering in candidate development. *Rural Special Education Quarterly, 34*(1), 10–16.

Cochran-Smith, M. and Paris, C. L. (1995). Mentor and mentoring: Did Homer have it right. In J. Smyth (Ed), *Critical discourses in teacher development* (181–202). London, UK: Cassell.

Council for Accreditation of Educator Preparation (CAEP). (2013). *CAEP accreditation standards.* Washington, DC: Author.

Council for the Accreditation of Educator Preparation [CAEP]. (2014). *Advanced Program Standards.* Retrieved from https://caepnet.files.wordpress.com/2014/07/caep_standards_for_advanced_programs.pdf.

Cuenca, A., Schmeichel, M., Butler, B. M., Dinkelman, T., & Nichols Jr, J. R. (2011). Creating a "third space" in student teaching: Implications for the university supervisor's status as outsider. *Teaching and Teacher Education, 27*(7), 1068–77.

Feiman-Nemser, S. (1998). Teachers as teacher educators. *European Journal of Teacher Education, 21*(1), 63–74.

Feiman-Nemser, S. (2001). Helping novices learn to teach: Lessons from an exemplary support teacher. *Journal of Teacher Education, 52*, 17–30.

Fisher, T. R. & Many, J. E. (2014). From PDS classroom teachers to urban teacher educators: Learning from professional development school boundary spanners. *School-University Partnerships, 7*(1), 49–63.

Hall, K. M., Draper, R. J., Smith, L. K., & Bullough, R. V. (2008). More than a place to teach: Exploring the perceptions of the roles and responsibilities of mentor teachers. *Mentoring & Tutoring: Partnership in Learning, 16*(3), 328–45.

Hobson, A. J., Ashby, P., Malderez, A., & Tomlinson, P. D. (2009). Mentoring beginning teachers: What we know and what we don't. *Teaching and Teacher Education, 25*(1), 207–16.

The Holmes Group (2007). *The Holmes Partnership trilogy: Tomorrow's teachers, tomorrow's schools, tomorrow's schools of education.* New York, NY: Peter Lang Publishing, Inc.

Hudson, P. (2013). Strategies for mentoring pedagogical knowledge. *Teachers and Teaching: Theory and Practice, 19*, 363–381. doi:10.1080/13540602.2013.770226.

Hudson, P., & Hudson, S. (2010). Mentor educators' understandings of mentoring preservice primary teachers. *International Journal of Learning, 17*(2), 157–69.

Ikpeze, C. H., Broikou, K. A., Hildenbrand, S., & Gladstone-Brown, W. (2012). PDS collaboration as Third Space: An analysis of the quality of learning experiences in a PDS partnership. *Studying Teacher Education, 8*(3), 275–88.

Lavadenz, M., & Hollins, E. (2015). Urban schools as settings for learning teaching. In E. Hollins (Ed.), *Rethinking field experiences in preservice teacher education* (1–14). New York, NY: Routledge.

Martin, S.D., Snow, J. L., & Franklin Torrez, C. A. (2011). Navigating the terrain of Third Space: Tensions with/in relationships in school-university partnerships. *Journal of Teacher Education, 62*(3), 299–311.

National Association for Professional Development Schools (2008). *What it means to be a professional development school.* Retrieved from http://napds.org/wp-content/uploads/2014/10/Nine-Essentials.pdf.

National Council for Accreditation of Teacher Education (2010). *Transforming teacher education through clinical practice: A national strategy to prepare effective teachers. Report of the Blue Ribbon Panel on clinical preparation and partnerships for improved learning.* Washington, DC: Author.

Norman, P. J., & Feiman-Nemser, S. (2005). Mind activity in teaching and mentoring. *Teaching and Teacher Education, 21*, 679–97.

Orland-Barak, L., & Klein, S. (2005). The expressed and the realized: Mentors' representation of a mentoring conversation and its realization in practice. *Teaching and Teacher Education, 21*, 379–402.

Parker, A. K., Zenkov, K., & Dennis, D. V. (2019). Exploring the lexicon or lack thereof in clinical teacher preparation. *Action in Teacher Education, 41*(3), 249–64. DOI: 10.1080/01626620.2019.1600601.

Parker, A.K., Zenkov, K., & Glaser, H. (under review). Preparing school-based teacher educators to serve as mentors: Maximizing clinical practice and PDS partnerships. Submitted to *Peabody Journal of Education.*

Richter, D., Kunter, M., Ludtke, O., Klusmann, U., Anders, Y., & Baumert, J. (2013). How different mentoring approaches affect beginning teachers' development in the first years of practice. *Teaching and Teacher Education, 36*, 166–77.

Richmond, G., Bartell, T., & Floden, R. (2017). Core teaching practices: Addressing both social justice and academic subject matter. *Journal of Teacher Education, 68*(5), 432–34.

Rochielle, J., & Carpenter, B. S. (2015). Navigating the third space. *Journal of Curriculum and Pedagogy, 12*(2), 131–33.

Russell, M. L., & Russell, J. A. (2011). Mentoring relationships: Cooperating teachers' perspectives on mentoring student interns. *Professional Educator, 35*(1), 16–35.

Rutherford, J. (1990). *Identity: Community, culture, difference*. London: Lawrence & Wishart.

Saldana, J. (2016). *The coding manual for qualitative researchers* (3rd ed.). Los Angeles, CA: Sage.

Sawyer, R. D., Neel, M. A., Coulter, M. (2016). At the crossroads of clinical practice and teacher leadership: A changing paradigm for professional practice. *International Journal of Teacher Leadership, 7*(1), 17–36.

Schatz-Oppenheimer, O. (2017). Being a mentor: Novice teachers' mentors' conceptions of mentoring prior to training. *Professional Development in Education, 343*(2), 274–92.

Schneider, J. (2018). Marching forward, marching in circles: A history of problems and dilemmas in teacher preparation. *Journal of Teacher Education, 69*(4), 330–40.

Soja, E. W. (1996). *Thirdspace: Journeys to Los Angeles and other real-and-imagined places*. Malden, MA: Blackwell.

Ulvik, M., & Sunde, E. (2013). The impact of mentor education: Does mentor education matter? *Professional Development in Education, 39*(5), 754–70.

Valencia, S. W., Martin, S. D., Place, N. A., & Grossman, P. (2009). Complex interactions in student teaching: Lost opportunities for learning. *Journal of Teacher Education, 60*(3), 304–22.

van Ginkel, G., Verloop, N., & Denessen, E. (2016). Why mentor? Linking mentor teachers' motivations to their mentoring conceptions. *Teachers and Teaching, 22*(1), 101–16.

Williams, J. (2014). Teacher educator professional learning in the Third Space. *Journal of Teacher Education 65*(4), 315–26.

Yendol-Hoppey, D., Dana, N. F., & Delane, D. C. (2009). Inquiry-oriented mentoring in the Professional Development School. *School-University Partnerships, 3*(1), 6–13.

Zeichner, K. (2013). The turn once again toward practice-based teacher education. *Journal of Teacher Education, 63*(5), 376–82.

Zeichner, K., & Bier, M. (2015). Opportunities and pitfalls in the turn toward clinical experience in U.S. teacher education. In E. R. Hollins (Ed.), *Rethinking field experiences in preservice teacher preparation: meeting new challenges for accountability* (20–46). New York: Routledge.

Zenkov, K., Parker, A. K., Parsons, S., Pellegrino, A., & Pytash, K. (2017). From project-based clinical experiences to collaborative inquiries: Pathways to Professional Development Schools. In J. Ferrara, J. Nath, I. Guadarrama, & R. Beebe (Eds.), *Expanding opportunities to link research and clinical practice: A volume in Research in Professional Development Schools* (9–33). Charlotte, NC: Information Age Publishing.

Zenkov, K. & Pytash, K. (2018). Critical, project-based clinical experiences: Their origins and their elements. In K. Zenkov & K. Pytash (Eds.), *Clinical experiences in teacher education: Critical, project-based experiences in diverse classrooms* (1–17). New York: Routledge.

Chapter Two

The Teacher Educators and Mentors (TEAM) Model

A Full-Year Clinical Residency Program

Amy Vessel, EdD, and Dawn Basinger, EdD,
Louisiana Tech University

The day-to-day work of a classroom teacher is complex and challenging, as is the work to recruit and prepare Louisiana's next generation of teachers. Beginning in 2014, as part of a long-term body of work to improve teacher preparation in Louisiana, the Louisiana Department of Education (LDoE) engaged K–12 educators, as well as schools, school systems, and teacher preparation leaders across the state to gather their feedback on teacher preparation experiences and how they can be strengthened.

In July 2014, the LDoE surveyed teachers statewide to inquire about their personal experiences with teacher preparation and classroom teaching. Principals and personnel directors shared experiences of hiring and supporting new teachers, and preparation program faculty shared their experiences collaborating with partner schools and school systems. Survey results highlighted some of the ongoing challenges facing teacher preparation programs and reported ideas from educators as to how school systems and preparation programs can collaborate to improve teacher preparation for future teacher-candidates.

In direct response to this feedback, the LDoE launched Believe and Prepare, which provided $4.89 million in grant funds to three cohorts of school systems to support closer partnerships between preparation providers and school system leaders to offer aspiring teachers a full year of practice under an expert mentor and a competency-based curriculum. Although three cohorts were to be funded in 2014, seven school systems and seven preparation providers were funded.

In 2015, the program grew to over twenty school systems and over fifteen preparation providers in Cohort 2, and in 2016, Cohort 3 consisted of over thirty school systems and over twenty preparation providers. In three years, over 850 undergraduate teacher-candidates were supported by expert mentors while pursuing certification through a yearlong residency program.

With a long-held vision of high-quality field experiences connected to theory and practice, faculty at Louisiana Tech University's College of Education were more than prepared to charter a path in the early years of the Louisiana State Department of Education's Believe and Prepare Initiative (2014). In fall 2014, the college's clinical director initiated a pilot residency program that included eleven elementary students, two elementary schools, and one school district. Currently, there are clinical residents in all teacher preparation programs, including traditional undergraduate and alternative certification, from early childhood through secondary teacher preparation programs in fifteen schools across twelve school districts.

After more than a decade of clinical work in area schools working alongside school leaders and mentors, the executive director of the Clinical Residency & Recruitment Center (CRRC) joined the former director of clinical experiences to transform the traditional student teaching program into a full-year residency model that included consistent and intentional support for school residency teams. In the spring of 2015, the Teacher Educators and Mentors (TEAM) Model was developed to facilitate this new approach to teacher preparation.

The model continues to evolve as early childhood, elementary, middle, and secondary undergraduate teacher preparation programs are redesigned using a competency-based framework published by the LDoE in 2016 after the Board of Elementary and Secondary Education adopted them in the same year. Louisiana Tech University's master of arts in teaching (MAT) alternative pathway programs are also aligning to the TEAM Model approach.

Louisiana Tech's teacher preparation program follows the Louisiana Department of Education requirements: Elementary, grades 1–5, residents are at their TEAM schools 80 percent (four days/week) of the time from August–May, completing more than 1,000–1,500 clinical hours during their senior year in the four-year undergraduate program. Middle, grades 4-8; Secondary, grades 6-12; and All-Level (K-12) residents are required to spend a minimum of 60 percent (three days/week) participation in schools during the fall and winter, and 80 percent (four days per week) participation during the spring. (LDoE, Updated Teacher Preparation Transition Guide, December 2017, p. 13).

In October 2016, the Louisiana Board of Elementary and Secondary Education (BESE), with support from the Louisiana Board of Regents (BoR), adopted landmark regulations to expand yearlong residencies (Louisiana State BESE, Bulletin 996, Revised August 2019). Early research on effective residencies (2017) identified the importance of recruitment, strong preparation, ongoing support, and higher teacher retention (Guha, Hyler, & Darling-Hammond). These anchors, along with additional clinical research (Bacharach & Heck, 2012; Danielson, 2015; Wilson, 2006), informed the development of the TEAM Model.

The following will provide insight into the evolution of a traditional student teaching program into a full-year teacher residency program. The chapter will address key components of the TEAM Model, residency program benefits, and recommendations for those redesigning their teacher preparation program.

COMPONENTS OF THE TEAM MODEL

The TEAM Model is much more than an extended student teaching experience. This new program stretches the co-teaching experience across a greater time frame, allowing clinical residents time to process clinical coaching to inform best practices for improvement. If some things take more time to grow, this slower pace of professional growth alleviates the stressful, short timetable of traditional student teaching.

The full-year residency model provides time and opportunity for more deeply educating teacher-candidates, or what the program refers to as clinical resident. In this more holistic approach to teacher preparation, clinical residents are able to engage in activities that "cultivate their capacity to teach with greater consciousness, self-awareness, and integrity" (Intrator & Kunzman, 2006, p. 39).

If future teachers are not prepared to address individual and cultural differences in addition to demonstrating content knowledge and instructional skills, then teacher preparation programs may be inadequately preparing the whole teacher to teach the whole student (Leonard & Basinger, 2008). While some aspects of the residency originated from traditional student teaching, others were created based upon teacher preparation and clinical residency research as well as school and district needs.

REDESIGNED CLINICAL COMPONENTS

TEAM roles. Influenced by the traditional student teaching triad (Yee, 1968), the TEAM Model provides a stronger foundation with multiple stakeholders,

Table 2.1. TEAM Model Roles

Teams	Roles
University Team	clinical director, clinical residency and recruitment center (CRRC) coordinator/clinical liaison, program faculty, university leadership team
District Team	district liaison(s), district supervisors, district leadership team
School Team	lead mentor-teacher, mentor-teachers, special education mentor(s), school leadership team
Residency Team	lead resident, residency team

which in turn increases better support and sustainability. The TEAM roles reflect an expanded version of the traditional student teaching triad of cooperating teacher, student-teacher, and university supervisor. Table 1 provides a visual representation of these roles according to their affiliation: university team, district team, school team, and resident team.

The university-based teacher educator team, or university team, includes the clinical director, who oversees early field experiences and clinical experiences in all initial certification programs, and a coordinator, who manages the CRRC and also serves as the clinical liaison. It is relevant to note that the liaison role was originally assigned to multiple teacher educators, many of whom had retired, who were assigned to a school or district. Now, faculty in the Curriculum, Instruction, and Leadership Department serve in multiple facets of the model from guest speakers to evaluators and to coaches as needed. The university leadership team consists of the clinical director, department chair, associate dean, and dean.

The district team consists of one or more liaisons, district supervisors, and a district leadership team (superintendent, HR director, liaison, etc.). The school team has a designated lead mentor-teacher, other mentor-teachers, a minimum of one special education mentor-teacher, and a school leadership team (typically the principal, vice principal, and sometimes a curriculum coordinator or strategist housed at the clinical setting).

This team reports the individual progress of each resident to the district and university through scheduled communication and TEAM reports. Expectations include regular walkthroughs in all TEAM classrooms, annual state-approved teacher evaluations, and summative recommendations for initial teacher certification.

The residency team is a very important aspect of the model, offering a cohort of peers/residents who are all pursuing initial teacher certification in the same academic year. Face-to-face meetings, as well as Zoom meetings, are conducted throughout the academic year, bringing this team together to collaborate, reflect, and discuss their professional growth as a group. These experiences are critical to the professional development of effective communication as well as preparing the whole teacher.

All clinical residents are placed in a clinical setting with at least one additional resident. Over time, a clear leader is identified and honored by the clinical director with the title of *lead resident* serving as the key contact of that team. In the table above, a residency team may have as many as six teacher educators coaching them over a full academic year.

Clinical liaison. While the TEAM Model organizational chart has gone through various changes as a result of various pilots over the years, one key role, the clinical liaison, has served an important role within clinical partnerships. That role was adapted from the University of Alabama's Clinical Master Teacher Model (Wilson, 2006; Daane, 2012).

Clinical liaisons represent the university and teacher educator teams in making the best decisions, communicating regularly, and meeting throughout the year as needed to make adjustments in placements and any policy changes. Most importantly, the liaisons hold all TEAM members accountable for meeting the expectations of their role in the residency program.

In the early stages of the TEAM Model, each school district had one grant-funded clinical liaison. Now, each district funds its own liaison. As the program has grown and expanded across the state into multiple districts and schools, the university created a budget line for one university clinical liaison to communicate and support each school-based team.

Office redesign. The CRRC was established in fall 2015 as a resource center for all members of the TEAM, and it continues to support TEAM members through educational programming, conferences, celebrations, community service, and social media. The clinical director and the university liaison are housed in this physical space on campus. A clinical classroom is provided across the hall for all mentor training, professional development, and clinical classes and consultations.

The center's website, latechcrrc.org, is the hub of communication. The website houses clinical resources for TEAM members to use, and each clinical partnership team has a page to spotlight successes. The CRRC was initially funded as part of a Louisiana Department of Education grant. The grant provided time for university leaders to review the current clinical experiences budget, reprioritize funding needs, and establish a new system for funding residencies.

Additional support was provided during the transition years by BESE in the form of an annual mentor and resident stipend. In 2019–2020, BESE continued to provide mentor stipends, but each district committed to resident stipends paid in two installments (December and May). This collaborative funding by all TEAM members has allowed sustainability for the program.

Clinical partnerships. Developing rich clinical partnerships through constant communication has been a key to this statewide initiative to improve teacher preparation programs and provide a pipeline for new teachers in Louisiana. Louisiana Tech University was one of three pilot programs that grew from one to twelve clinical partnerships across the I-20 Corridor of North Louisiana in five years.

Memorandum of Understandings (MOUs) are a growing educational trend for all collaborative projects, and MOUs are signed annually between the university and each district detailing expectations of each party. Discussions of the upcoming academic year begin six months prior to the beginning of the new school year, and leaders from both entities sign the formal documentation after annual partnership meeting discussions, clarifications, etc.

Partnerships have existed for decades with many school districts, but the collaboration, communication, and joint ventures have increased each year. New districts from across the state contact the university to begin partnership discussions. Leadership teams from each district meet to share goals, prepare MOUs, establish partnerships supporting residencies, grant projects, teacher recruitment, and more.

Mentor training. Research demonstrates that mentor training is essential for successful clinical experiences (Sutcher, Darling-Hammond, & Carver-Thomas, 2016; Vessel, 2005). In 2015–2016, TEAM Model mentor training was provided by the authors, and more than one hundred school-based teacher educators attended. Mentor training curriculum was collaboratively designed, including research-based strategies from the St. Cloud Co-Teaching Model, Roles of the TEAM, Full-Year Residency Best Practices, the Danielson Framework/TEAM Evaluation, Generational Differences, and Clinical Coaching.

To date, more than four hundred mentors have been trained across twelve partnerships. Three years ago, the state began a nine-day state mentor training and now provides an ancillary certificate for mentors that requires the completion of a portfolio assessment. This state training is in addition to the training already offered by the CRRC. Louisiana Tech University is currently the only university in the state to be approved to offer both mentor and content leader professional development for state educators, and all training is provided online with face-to-face optional learning opportunities. While required state certification emphasizes the importance of the role of mentor, TEAM training with all new mentors will remain a priority as state training is more generalized to all types of mentoring.

RESIDENCY MODEL: ESSENTIAL COMPONENTS

TEAM school growth. The model established a protocol with each new district beginning with two distinct clinical settings: one elementary TEAM school and one secondary TEAM school. In the past five years, some districts have grown to more than one elementary, secondary, or middle school clinical setting, but many have built a strong foundation in the original TEAM school.

To establish a TEAM of teacher-candidates and school-based educators, a minimum of two candidates should be at one school site. For example, during the 2018–2019 academic year, there were twelve school districts and twenty-one schools. One district had one K–8 TEAM school supporting both elementary and middle/secondary teacher-candidates, while another district had six TEAM schools: three elementary, one middle school, and two high schools.

In one urban district, three residents began at the designated elementary school, and two began at the designated high school. Now, four years later, the elementary school boasts seven residents where one alumna is successfully teaching and serving as a mentor. At the high school, numbers have tripled hosting six residents this year in four secondary programs (mathematics, science, health and physical education, and English). Because English residents requested the same district, a second TEAM high school to be identified by the stakeholders. At mid-term, all three TEAM schools are thriving, and the new school has received some extra attention as all members are learning the accountability system.

Residents' geographic locations influence their placements. Many choose to return to their home, and the districts seek these residents hoping they will choose to remain in that district after their residency. Districts are excited to have the entire academic year to know the resident's knowledge, skills, and dispositions and determine if they are the right fit for its schools. In another very strong partnership, there was one year with no residents, simply due to the geographical location. Rural districts, especially, are providing incentives such as mileage and additional stipends to recruit them. Recruiting continues to have a clear alignment to residents' future hiring preferences.

Full-year co-teaching environment. Building upon St. Cloud State University's Co-Teaching Model (Bacharach, Heck, & Dahlberg, 2010) and its professional development sessions, Louisiana Tech University's College of Education provides its own development opportunities. Teacher-candidates and mentor-teachers participate in co-planning, co-teaching, and co-assessment training that is expected to be used throughout the academic year.

In addition, teacher-candidates and mentor-teachers receive professional development for collaboration in instructional teams and student achievement strategies. Adaptations were made to the co-teaching model to accommodate a full-year residency schedule within the university's quarter system. Both the resident and mentor-teacher seem to thrive in this environment, even making evaluations less stressful.

A TEAM approach to evaluation. Multiple summative and formative evaluations are conducted throughout the entire academic year to measure growth and ensure the success of all clinical residents, including a team approach to quarterly reporting. The TEAM is trained to use the nationally recognized Danielson Framework for Teaching Tool (FFT) (2015), as the primary formal evaluation tool, with crosswalks to other national standards (i.e., INTASC, CLASS, TAP, etc.). The FFT is introduced to teacher-candidates early in the program and used as the evaluation instrument during practicum and residency. It is also an integral part of the training that mentor-teachers participate in before and during the clinical residency.

Resident evaluations occur in fall (August–November), winter (December–February), and spring (March–May). Similar to medical or other professional programs, teacher-candidates complete three clinical rotations, or residencies, mastering the skills of an effective teacher from August to May. During each quarter, a team of two to three mentor-teachers and university faculty observe and provide feedback as the resident provides evidence of professional growth. Such coaching by the mentor-teachers has shown to be an empowering experience (Wilson, 2006; Daane, 2012).

The resident also completes a self-assessment, and all school leaders commit to complete the state-approved teacher evaluation. The protocol for clinical evaluations begins as early as the sophomore year in methodology and practicum courses and includes a pre-conference form, lesson plan, post-conference form, and actionable feedback conference form. University faculty are involved in all aspects of clinical coaching, from professionalism to specific content. Informal feedback protocols are additionally available for all TEAM members.

Recent clinical research supports digitally mediated supervision in the form of self-reflection, walkthroughs, focused feedback, and formal evaluation (Hodges & Baum, 2019). The addition of SWIVL technology to the TEAM Model in the fall of 2018 bridged the gap as the program was able to grow beyond a sixty-mile radius. A customized account allows all residents to *tag* their videos with any of Danielson's classroom management and instructional indicators. This process makes it very easy for the clinical coaches to locate the evidence, and it is highly beneficial to the residents as they learn the four domains of teaching associated with the Danielson Framework.

Communication via technology. Danielson (2015) emphasized the importance of communication during the clinical coaching process of teacher preparation: "Conversations about teaching occur between teaching partners; between teachers and their mentors, coaches, or supervisors; and within teaching teams or professional learning communities" (Danielson, 2015, p. 38). Team conversations are critical and take place constantly between all stakeholders. Technology is greatly assisting the growth of clinical partnerships across the state. All clinical video evaluations are captured by SWIVL technology.

All clinical documentation is paperless, captured by Survey Monkey and Google Doc tools. Clinical liaison meetings were originally face-to-face, but they are now recorded through Zoom video conferences. Communication trees were originally on the Group Me, but have changed to other app options, such as Band. Using communication via technology has saved time and money.

Mentor selection and placements. Determining the best match of mentor-teacher to clinical resident is essential in making a full-year clinical placement. For that reason, a timeline begins with the mid-year recruitment event in January, where all clinical partners have the opportunity to meet upcoming residents. Faculty audit candidates' plans of study to determine eligibility before candidate applications are submitted.

In the state of Louisiana, residency certificates are now required for all candidates before the beginning of the residency. In early spring, university and district clinical partnership meetings take place, mentor-teachers are recommended by both the university and school partners, and TEAM schools are identified. Training begins for residents and mentors in late spring, and placements are typically finalized in the summer months.

The district and university leaders take much time and care in determining the best mentors to serve for the upcoming residency program. Purposeful matching of the mentor and resident is essential for a successful nine-month co-teaching collaboration. A clinical style inventory has been piloted for a few years to support quality, purposeful matching of residents to mentors for the full-year residency experience.

Initial results have shown that common traits in the mentor and resident have caused an increase in earlier co-planning, co-teaching, and co-assessment. In addition to the mid-year recruiting event, the CRRC hosts other recruitment events.

Recruitment events. The center hosts a variety of special events throughout the academic year to spotlight and bring prestige to the teaching profession. These have become part of a recruiting effort to engage middle school, high school, and potential college transfer students to consider teaching. Every fall, Dot Day is celebrated, adapted from Peter Reynolds (2003) award-winning children's book, *The Dot*, where all TEAM members, students, faculty, alumni, and friends join together to celebrate educators *making their mark* in this world!

CRRC also hosts a recruiting event, Taste of the TEAM, throughout the year, and, by a school request, for middle or high school students who may want to become a teacher. Students from partner districts travel to Louisiana Tech University in school buses. Students tour the CRRC, classrooms, library, and the lab school, where they meet faculty, current teacher preparation students, and clinical residents.

In the spring, with an invitation to family and friends, clinical residents are recognized for completing their program and honored with the distinction of a clinical fellow. The authors believe that its residents deserve this distinction after investing an entire year in a clinical experience. University and district leaders, faculty, and mentor-teachers also attend the event. As previously discussed, Louisiana began to pilot full-year residencies in fall 2014. Universities and school districts continue to work collaboratively to recruit future teachers and prepare them for the workforce.

Professional development, ongoing support, and financial honorariums are available to mentors who want to mentor residents through best practices in a co-teaching environment. Communication and meetings facilitated by technology, addressing the whole teacher, collaborating, co-teaching, and sharing resources and data all provide a rich foundation for the sustainability of the TEAM Model. These efforts are helping all to meet the common goal to provide a high-quality teacher workforce for students now and in the future.

BENEFITS TO ALL STAKEHOLDERS

While the transition from student teaching to the residency program has not been without its challenges, there have been several mutually beneficial success stories that are too noteworthy not to share. These include improved university/district partnerships, increased classroom instructional time, meeting district workforce needs, empowering mentors, and ensuring the success of teacher-candidates as they begin their teaching careers.

Improved University/District Partnerships

In more than fifty years of partnerships, communication and collaboration are stronger than ever. Districts routinely contact us to inquire about the new pool of teachers, to collaborate on funding opportunities, and to discuss proposed or new state policies. The College of Education has increased district membership in its curriculum, policy, and assessment committees. Both the college and districts strive to share resources and professional development opportunities. University faculty attend district events and many of district partners serve as guest speakers or adjunct instructors. Great partnerships are one benefit for all stakeholders. Another is increased classroom instruction and practice for clinical residents.

Instructional Time

Teacher residency programs show great promise in improving preservice preparation and strengthening early-career mentoring. Residents experience the beginning of school, the beginning and end of multiple instructional units, and the impact their teaching strategies have on their students. Residents have the time to internalize what they are learning as well as what their students are learning through this extended time to practice. Extended instructional time also means more time for the clinical resident to better understand one's strengths, areas for development, and who they want to be as a teacher.

Beginning in July 2018, a teacher-candidate serving in a BESE-approved yearlong residency must hold a resident teacher certificate. Because residents hold a provisional certificate and are in most cases the appropriate substitute for the mentor-teacher, the state allows them to substitute for their mentor-teachers. Per Bulletin 996, "Holders of the resident teacher certificate may serve as a substitute teacher in their residency school system for up to ten days each semester" (Section 328, G; retrieved from Louisiana Department of Education, Teacher Preparation Transition Guide, 2017).

Mentors have commented on the ease of maintaining the scope and sequence of the curriculum with little to no need to reteach upon return to the classroom. School leaders love the built-in substitute teacher and wish there was a resident in every classroom at their school. Districts also have this extra time to evaluate and determine if they would like to hire the teacher resident.

Empowered Teachers

At the heart of the TEAM Model residency program is the mentor-teacher. From training to ancillary certificates, the mentor is a critical member of the TEAM. Their voices are critical to the success of the program as they commit to share every single aspect of their career with an apprentice, including their students and physical space. In the past five years, there has been a 97 percent retention rate of mentor-teachers in the TEAM Model. Those rotating out of the mentor role were promoted to school leader positions. Alumni of the TEAM Model received high scores on their annual teaching evaluations, with several being hired at the same site where they completed their residency.

The retention rate of those completing the residency is slightly higher than those completing a traditional student teaching experience. School leaders have compared TEAM Model first-year teachers to those traditionally prepared teachers in their fifth year of teaching, noting that clinical residents' knowledge and skills meet or exceed those traditionally prepared. Along with better preparation of clinical residents, student academic success is also higher.

Student Success

Districts are comparing TEAM Model classrooms to traditional classrooms, and there are indications of significant student growth. In addition, individual testimonies speak very favorably to the strength of two sets of eyes in the classroom to determine needs that might have otherwise gone unnoticed. Several mentors have mentioned that classroom management has been better.

Residents are truly making their mark and having a sustained impact. They have had the opportunity to co-lead professional development, sponsor science fairs, serve on the staff of a state championship football team, and directly or indirectly impact student achievement. For example, in August 2018, a teacher resident, not the mentor-teacher, determined that a student could not read a pre-test. Residents get to know the strengths and weaknesses of their students and provide them with additional academic assistance. Students are more engaged and put more effort into their work. Student success demands the whole teacher teaching the whole student.

RECOMMENDATIONS

With an estimated 316,000 teachers needed each year by 2025, teachers are in continuous demand (Sutcher, Darling-Hammond, & Carver-Thomas, 2016). A key characteristic aligned to teacher retention is strong mentorship (Heider, 2005). TEAM Model leaders are pursuing new and innovative ways through clinical partnerships to share data with area school districts to validate the TEAM Model through clinical research. For any program exploring a shift to a full-year residency from a more traditional one-semester student teaching experience, there are several recommendations that deserve thoughtful consideration.

Carefully Select Partnerships

It is critical to purposefully select. Likewise, school districts should be fully informed of the residency program before committing to partner with a teacher preparation program. The liaisons representing each entity must have a strong professional relationship built upon trust to move the partnership forward and see growth in the program. The reputation of the TEAM schools begins with a solid support system from resident stipends to professional development and regular school leader walkthroughs. Clinical residencies cannot occur without great district partners and continuous communication.

Start Small

The TEAM Model began in one district with nine clinical residents and grew slowly into districts where program needs were being met for both stakeholders. Diversity of district school sites were considered establishing urban, suburban, and rural TEAM schools. However, placements at a distance of fifty or more miles were challenging for clinical residents who still had coursework during the day.

Highly effective mentor-teachers were sought and recommended by district liaisons, but only one elementary and one high school in three districts was selected so the CRRC could support the growth as well as the management of a few TEAM Model schools. Not only was it a challenge for clinical residents and the CRRC, but mentor-teachers were also committing to invest in a resident for a full year.

Mentor-Teachers and School Leaders

Slowly determining the best mentor for each resident is important. The mentor-teacher must be willing to share all aspects of planning, teaching, and assessment. Some teachers, even teachers of the year, have a hard time giving up control. The co-teaching practices used in the TEAM Model do not require solo teaching time, but even sharing 50/50 is difficult for some educators.

The mentor-teacher may not teach all day in the content area needed by the teacher resident. For some teachers, they teach outside their content area or do not teach all day if serving in a school leadership capacity. Those educators may not be the best fit for a resident who needs a full day of teaching in their pursued certification area. The mentor-teacher must be an effective communicator.

While mentors may have the highest gains in student achievement from the previous year, they may not be able to talk through planning, teaching, and assessment strategies until they understand how to communicate to a different generation, that is, Generation X communicating with Generation Y or Z clinical residents. Initiating the TEAM Model is not only a challenge for the mentor-teacher, but it requires that school leaders buy in and support these practices.

Building and sustaining a team of mentors in one school requires strong school leadership. The school leader needs to have a clear understanding of the expectations of the TEAM Model for both mentor-teachers and teacher residents. When mentor-teachers started training, district and school leader(s) were also invited.

Mentor training is now facilitated through online courses and most, if not all, district and school leaders participated in initial training sessions. Upon reflection, those schools that exemplified the TEAM Model philosophy from the classroom to the administrative office, have all doubled in TEAM classrooms. Teacher preparation, mentor training, technology needs, etc., do come with a price.

Seek Financial Support During Transition

Many K–12 and higher education programs have seen budget cuts within the last five years. Additional funding will be critical as you start a full-year teaching residency. While the initiative discussed in this chapter was a state-initiated redesign, a proposal for funding still had to be submitted. As mentioned earlier, to sustain growth and build a strong foundation for a teacher residency, you will need financial support from your state, institution, or school districts.

If a traditional student teaching program covers one semester or fifteen weeks, a full-year residency might feel like two student teaching semesters. Transitioning from student teaching to clinical residency will require a complete transformation. You will need to reevaluate your assessment system, find additional financial support, and have stakeholder buy-in for this to work.

Adjust the Clinical Lens of Stakeholders

Superintendents, school leaders, mentors, residents, university clinical faculty, parents, and students must understand that a residency is not two student teaching experiences, but a longer timeframe for mastery of teaching knowledge and skills. The resident has more time to provide consistent evidence of planning, instruction, management, and professionalism from August to May. From the beginning, all stakeholders must understand the expectations of a full-year teaching residency.

In August, clinical residents attend the first in-service with their mentor-teacher. Then, they both have the opportunity to prepare the classroom for their students prior to the first day of school. School leaders should introduce the teacher resident as a co-teacher to all school employees. Every school employee, as well as parents, must acknowledge the teacher resident as a resident in practice, and in the case of Louisiana, each teacher resident holds a resident teacher certificate.

The school should display the teacher resident's name on the classroom door next to their mentor-teacher's name, extend a personal workplace for them, provide necessary resources, and support their professional development. Residents have mentioned that this is a key benefit of becoming part of the school culture. It is also a key advantage for all stakeholders, including college faculty, when implementing and sustaining the TEAM Model.

Re-Conceptualize Faculty Participation

Whereas traditional student teaching programs have been led by clinical directors and facilitated by university supervisors, many of whom were retired educators, the TEAM approach to full-year residencies has increased participation of college faculty. Early Childhood and Elementary/Special Education college faculty teach some of their classes in partner schools prior to residency and evaluate them during their residency.

However, to save on the cost of travel, as well as limiting the time away from the college, technology was utilized to facilitate all stages of the evaluation, pre-, face-to-face, and post-evaluations. In addition, with clinical residents spending more time in school classrooms, technology also helps to connect with them on a regular basis. Faculty, teachers, and residents have been using Swivl and ZOOM to facilitate these connections. Seeking new and innovative ways to keep that connection will be important.

College of Education faculty also serve as guest speakers at professional development meetings, serve as academic advisors, conduct clinical evaluations through Swivl, volunteer to provide expertise for residents in need of growth in specific areas, etc. Keeping the university team abreast of residents' growth throughout the academic year could be compared to K–12 school-level data meetings. Reviewing clinical data by program will be essential to the success of the residents and, when shared with all stakeholders, vital to the continuation of the TEAM Model.

Gather Feedback from Stakeholders

Seeking regular feedback from college faculty, district leaders, school leaders, mentors, and residents have strengthened the TEAM Model. From surveys to interviews to face-to-face meetings, the powerful data used to inform the development of the TEAM Model came directly from all participants over the past five years. Stakeholders outside of the college appreciate that their voices and suggestions are heard.

All stakeholders' feedback has inspired TEAM Model participants and improved teacher preparation programs, strengthened relations with district partners, and, hopefully, increased student achievement. None of this would be possible if change and flexibility were not embraced.

Maintain Flexibility

During a school year, circumstances and needs shift and change; flexibility is a requirement. For instance, mentor and teacher resident placements may change, district schools may rotate, district and college personnel may change, and budgets fluctuate from year to year if not during the academic year. The early years of piloting residencies were exciting and challenging. Having the flexibility to laugh in some situations and quickly problem-solve in others became essential skills for the clinical director.

Moving into an unknown realm of a full-year clinical experience was frustrating at times, but the voices from the classrooms encouraged the pursuit of a stronger preparation for future educators. Seek clinical and district leaders who are creative, flexible, and willing to try and try again when a new idea doesn't work. Initiating a full-year teacher residency will be the most frustrating and exciting time in that educator's career, but the determination to persevere will be the greatest reward as a new residency is established.

Share the Story

Don't be afraid to try new things, to ditch things that don't work, to learn from others, and to share the good along with the bad as you establish or change programs, procedures, and policies. Sharing the TEAM Model story has been a wonderful experience. So much has happened during these five years. Initially, stories were shared with prospective residents, college faculty, school district partners, and other institutions of higher education.

Then, with the establishment of a website, stories of success were shared, partnerships spotlighted, and news and other events posted. This website is still in use and has been a positive marketing tool for the entire university and community. Now, with this book chapter, the authors hope to reach many more educators who are interested in learning about the TEAM Model story.

REFERENCES

Bacharach, N., & Heck, T. W. (2012). Voices from the field. *Educational Renaissance*, *1*(1), 49–61.

Bacharach, N., Heck, T. W., & Dahlberg, K. (2010). Changing the face of student teaching through co-teaching. *Action in Teacher Education*, *32*(1), 3–14.

Daane, C. J. (2012). Clinical master teacher program: Teachers' and interns' perceptions of supervision with limited university intervention. *Action in Teacher Education*, *22*(1), 93–100.

Danielson, C. (2015). *The framework for teaching evaluation instrument.* Moorabbin VIC: Hawker Brownlow Education.

Danielson, C. (2015). Framing discussions about teaching. *Educational Leadership*, *72*(7), 38–41.

Guha, R., Hyler, M. E., & Darling-Hammond, L. (2017). The power and potential of teacher residencies. *Phi Delta Kappan*, *98*(8), 31–37.

Heider, K. L. (2005). Teacher isolation: How mentoring programs can help. *Current Issues in Education*, *8*(14).

Hodges, T. E., & Baum, A. C. (2019). *Handbook of research on field-based teacher education*. Hershey, PA: IGI Global, Information Science Reference.

Intrator, S. M., & Kunzman, R. (2006). Starting with the soul. *Educational Leadership*, *63*(6), 38–42.

Leonard, P., & Basinger, D. (2008). Educating the whole teacher. *The Beacon*, *4*(2), 1–8.

Louisiana Department of Education, Board of Secondary and Elementary Education (2019). *Standards for approval of teacher and educational leader preparation programs* (Bulletin 996).

Louisiana Department of Education (2014). *Partners in preparation: A survey of educators & education preparation programs.* Retrieved from https://www.louisianabelieves.com/docs/default-source/links-for-newsletters/partners-in-preparation-survey-report.pdf?sfvrsn=6.

Louisiana Department of Education: Believe and Prepare (2014). Retrieved from https://www.louisianabelieves.com/teaching/believe-and-prepare.

Louisiana Department of Education: Believe and Prepare (2016). *BESE expands full-year classroom residency for teachers.* Retrieved from https://www.louisianabelieves.com/newsroom/news-releases/2016/10/12/bese-expands-full-year-classroom-residency-for-teachers.

Louisiana Department of Education (2016). *Louisiana teacher preparation competencies.* Retrieved from https://www.louisianabelieves.com/docs/default-source/teaching/teacher-preparation-competencies.pdf?sfvrsn=4.

Louisiana Department of Education (2017). *Believe and prepare teacher preparation transition guide.* Retrieved from https://www.louisianabelieves.com/docs/defaul-source/teaching/teacher-preparation-transition-guide.pdf?sfvrsn=12.

National Education Association (2014). *Teacher residencies: Redefining preparation through partnerships.* Retrieved from https://files.eric.ed.gov/fulltext/ED575641.pdf.

National Council on Teacher Quality (2016). *Undergraduate elementary teacher prep review*. Retrieved from: https://www.nctq.org/review/search/program/1.

Reynolds, P. H. (2003). *The Dot.* Somerville, MA: Candlewick Press.

Sutcher, L., Darling-Hammond, L., & Carver-Thomas, D. (2019). Understanding teacher shortages: An analysis of teacher supply and demand in the United States. *Education Policy Analysis Archives, 27*(35).

Vessel, A. (2005). Defining the Role of Clinical School Faculty in Clinical Experiences: A Redesign of the Teacher Preparation Program, *Essays in Education, 14*(14).

Wilson, E. K. (2006). The impact of an alternative model of student-teacher supervision: Views of the participants. *Teaching and Teacher Education, 22*(1), 22–31.

Yee, A. H. (1968). Interpersonal relationships in the student-teaching triad. *Journal of Teacher Education, 19*(1), 95–112.

Chapter Three

A Model for Success
A Modified Yearlong Clinical Internship
Amy M. Rogers, PhD, and
Courtney A. Dexter, PhD, Lycoming College

Designing and maintaining a strong teacher preparation program is hard work. Central to creating high-quality programs are clinical components (Darling-Hammond, 2014), which require trusting relationships with schools and individuals. These relationships take time to develop collaborative partnerships, as well as meet the multiple demands of the variety of stakeholders, including accrediting bodies, professional organizations, state departments of education, local education associations, and the university faculty, staff, and students. Effective clinical teacher preparation can assume many forms.

This model, applicable to a variety of educator preparation programs, provides *all* teacher-candidates the opportunity to complete a modified yearlong clinical internship. Learning opportunities with a common mentor-teacher throughout a yearlong modified clinical internship help better prepare the teacher-candidate for a successful clinical internship. The purpose of this chapter is to outline the process used for a modified clinical internship for elementary, secondary, K–12, and dual certification with special education teacher-candidates. The guiding foundational frameworks, design and maintenance of the program, and how outcome data are used for program assessment are discussed and examined in detail.

GUIDING PRINCIPLES

The design of the preparation program is informed by research and theory on effective teacher preparation, specifically research on clinical internships

(American Association of Colleges for Teacher Education, 2010; Hammerness, Darling-Hammond, Grossman, Rust, & Shulman, 2005; Clark, Triggs, & Nielsen, 2014; Association of Teacher Education, 2019). Influenced by professional organizations such as ATE, AACTE, CEC, and CAEP, the development of the yearlong clinical model of teacher preparation mirrors that espoused by these organizations.

In the clinical model of teacher preparation, both school-based and university-based teacher educators commit to a level of interaction with teacher-candidates that demands sharing and applying their vast professional experience and acting as leaders to their aspiring colleagues (AACTE Clinical Practice Commission, 2018). *Mentor-teachers* are carefully selected and provide resources and learning opportunities to guide and support aspiring teacher-candidates over a yearlong period in the PK–12 classrooms.

Clinical practice refers to various field experiences a teacher-candidate participates in during the teacher preparation program, with the *clinical internship* referring to the culminating, professional semester of student teaching. To address both the importance and centrality of clinical preparation within teacher education programs, organizations such as the American Association of Colleges for Teacher Education (AACTE), Association of Teacher Educators (ATE), and Council for Accreditation of Education Association (CAEP) recently released reports supporting clinical preparation in teacher education (AACTE, 2018; ATE, 2016; CAEP, 2015).

To improve and refine Lycoming College's teacher preparation program, faculty consistently reflects on the effectiveness of the program using state and national standards. The hope is to provide a basic framework for comparable teacher preparation programs build, maintain, and sustain successful partnerships. It is recognized that the amount of time committed to clinical practices and internship by educator preparation programs varies from program to program.

Respectfully, each program knows what is best for their students and partner schools. The flexibility of programs to best meet the needs of local education associations (LEA) and university stakeholders is of utmost importance, allowing for local contextual variables to play a role in the sustainable and shared infrastructure.

PROGRAM DESCRIPTION

I Am Lycoming

Authors of this chapter are full-time, tenure-line faculty members in the Education Department at Lycoming College. Lycoming College is much more than a place; it is much more than a college. It is something the Lycoming community of students, faculty, and staff embrace and become. As education faculty at Lycoming, the authors are professors, advisors, professionals, researchers, coaches, mentors, and so much more.

Founded in 1812, Lycoming College is a traditional, four-year, private, liberal arts and sciences college dedicated to the undergraduate education of approximately 1,200–1,300 students. Rigorous, twenty-first-century academics, vibrant residential communities (approximately 86 percent of students reside on campus), and supportive faculty foster widely successful student outcomes. Considered a Tier One National Liberal Arts College by the *U.S. News & World Report* (Lycoming College Rankings, 2019), Lycoming offers students a first-rate liberal arts and sciences education, with the learning environment characterized by intensive, meaningful, and frequent student-faculty interaction.

Meet the Team

The Education Department truly embraces the liberal arts tradition by offering a wide variety of enriching academic experiences and opportunities to explore a liberal arts major in addition to teacher certification. Approximately one hundred students are enrolled in the teacher certification program, seeking a variety of certification areas. In order to make a successful program, Lycoming College partners with several LEAs in the community. A vital part of a successful partnership between LEAs and Institutions of Higher Education (IHEs) are sustainable and shared infrastructure (AACTE, 2018).

Faculty. Currently, three tenure-line faculty members, holding PhD or EdD degrees, comprise the Education faculty at Lycoming. Each faculty member is vested in the success of the teacher-candidates and wears multiple hats as part of the departmental obligations and responsibilities. Education at Lycoming is not a major or minor but a special program. All courses offered by the education faculty have a clinical practice component with a minimum of twenty hours per semester.

With each clinical practice, including the culminating pre-clinical and internship, faculty members connect theory to practice through class discussion, assignments, and evaluation. The design, duration, and intensity of the clinical practice varies, yet the focus remains on connecting theory to practice and fostering the learning of both students and faculty.

Director of teacher education and chief certification officer. An education faculty member serves in this role, with course reduction for responsibilities related to this position. They are responsible for offering primary guidance to the field placement coordinator and clinical supervisors, as well as serving as the primary contact for post-baccalaureate and intern candidates.

Additional duties include serving as the IHE certifying officer responsible for (1) verifying teacher-candidates for certification (exit interviews with each intern, graduation date, program evaluation, successful PECT and Praxis test completion, qualitative data related to whether the candidate is "of good moral character," analysis of the state department teacher-candidate evaluation form), (2) teacher-candidate evaluation documentation on the state department teacher-candidate evaluation form, and (3) certifying successful completion of all departmental requirements.

Student teaching/clinical supervisor. Two full-time supervisors provide pedagogical and content support, in addition to supervising, coaching, and evaluating teacher-candidates and pre-practicum students. Serving as a liaison between partner schools and the Education Department, the supervisors communicate program expectations and provide individual trainings with mentor-teachers, establish measurable goals, and plan biweekly observations.

The supervisors also inform and collaborate with the director of teacher education, field placement coordinator, and education faculty by providing weekly updates on each of the teacher-candidates in their pre-clinical and clinical internship. As a member of the education department team, the supervisors attend monthly faculty meetings and are an integral part of departmental decisions related to teacher training and planning of events.

Lastly, supervisors serve as teaching faculty who lead seminars for the cohort of teacher-candidates in pre-practicum clinical and weekly seminar for the teacher interns who are in their clinical internship semester. Weekly seminars are held on campus, at partner schools, and on the Intermediate Unit 17 (BLaST) campus. Topics include data analysis, special education, classroom technology, résumé and cover letter building, STEM, professional evaluation models, college and career readiness, and PA Future Ready Index.

Field placement coordinator. The primary responsibilities of the field placement coordinator are to plan, prepare, and coordinate the placement of all levels of clinical practice, including the yearlong clinical internship. The coordinator is responsible for working with partner schools on the selection of highly effective field and mentor-teachers and working closely with the director of teacher education.

Department faculty, clinical supervisors, and the field placement coordinator hold formal interviews with teacher-candidates entering into the semester prior to their yearlong clinical internship. Questions related to field experiences, challenges associated with the professional semester, state and program requirement updates, and preference for location of clinical internship are explored.

Mentor-teacher. If a teacher-candidate is seeking dual certification in elementary or secondary and special education, the clinical internship is split between two mentor-teachers in their respective certification areas. Requirements to serve as a mentor-teacher in Pennsylvania include: (a) at least three years of satisfactory teaching experience; (b) one year of certified experience in the school entity where the intern is assigned; (c) certification in the subject competency of the teacher-candidate; and (d) mentor training by the institution (PDE, 2012).

Additionally, Lycoming College works with LEA coordinators to identify mentor-teachers with established disposition profiles of being positive role models, excellent classroom managers, engaging educators, reflective practitioners, and motivated mentors who are willing to support and direct a teacher-candidate's professional development.

I Am Becoming an Educator

Lycoming College provides programs for many teaching certificates in the areas of general education and special education. One such effort is the modified yearlong clinical internship, as represented in figure 3.1.

The yearlong partnership between teacher-candidate and the mentor-teacher allows sufficient time and opportunity to address challenges that may arise or, in seldom cases, change placement if necessary. As with many teacher preparation programs, there are challenges, such as competition with nearby universities, providing ample stipends to the mentor-teachers, and meeting the demands of changes in state mandates.

However, specific issues related to changes in the placement for the modified yearlong clinical internship include, but are not limited to, a significant personality conflict between the mentor and teacher-candidate, the mentor-teacher being moved to a different classroom or assuming an administrative position, and the mentor-teacher taking a leave of absence or not returning for personal reasons. Through meaningful partnerships in clinical settings, the teacher-candidates work with both university and mentor-teachers as they learn to connect theory and practice and develop into effective educators.

SECURE PLACEMENT

Teacher-candidates engage in an application process prior to being place in their yearlong modified clinical internship. This includes securing at least two favorable recommendations from individuals outside the Education Department, submitting transcripts, and participating in an interview with education faculty, supervisors, and placement coordinator. The interview discussion consists of the teacher-candidate's previous experiences in educational

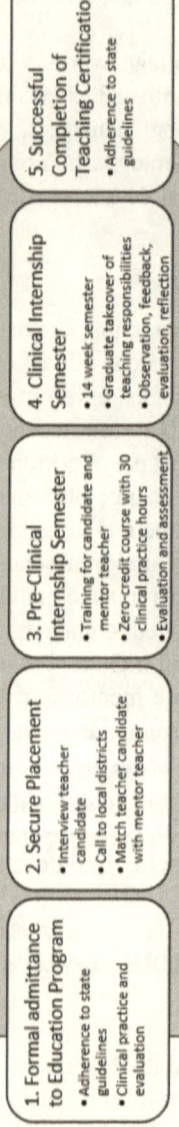

Figure 3.1. Process of Formal Admittance to Completion of Teaching Certification

settings, skills and knowledge obtained through their progress in the program, areas of strengths and needs, and placement preferences.

Based on this information and experiences with teacher-candidates, brief writeups detailing relevant information about each candidate were constructed, including specific needs and requirements and responsibilities of the mentor-teachers. The field placement coordinator submits a brief bio of each teacher-candidate to the appropriate school district administrator responsible for working with universities in order to best match teacher-candidates and mentor-teachers.

Depending on the process of the LEA (e.g., one-on-one recommendation, list of potential mentor-teachers, email correspondence), the LEA administrator and the Education Department team work together to narrow down possibilities for a successful match between teacher-candidate and mentor-teacher. Students pursuing dual certification in general and special education or any of the K–12 certification areas (art, music, modern language) will likely have split placements. Formal letters securing each placement are distributed to the district, school, and mentor-teacher, and arrangements are made for stipends for the mentor-teachers for hosting Lycoming College teacher-candidates.

PRE-CLINICAL INTERNSHIP SEMESTER

Teacher-candidates are notified of their clinical internship placement in the first few weeks of the pre-clinical internship semester. Clinical supervisors meet individually with mentor-teachers at least two times for one-on-one training on the nature of the pre-clinical practice, expectations, supervision skills, roles and responsibilities, and evaluation methods. They are provided digital and manual access to the teacher education handbook and other resources needed to begin working with the teacher-candidate.

Major components of this pre-internship semester include participating in a zero-credit course (Pre-Student Teaching Practicum) taught by the clinical supervisors and completing a minimum of thirty hours in their clinical internship placement(s). EDUC 348 includes a series of course meetings over the sixteen-week semester and includes a dedicated topic and qualified speaker, with reflection and application activities to follow. A sampling of topics recently covered include digital footprint and building social media profile, the Danielson Framework and reflection, classroom management, and connection and communication.

An item of particular significance in this pre-internship semester is each candidate developing their student teaching portfolio. Historically, this has been in binder form but now, teacher candidates in addition to the traditional binder, create an online portfolio to meet the needs of LEAs and their application/hiring processes.

Required content of the binder is consistently reviewed and updated to align with the needs of the field. For example, a section with materials targeted toward students with exceptionalities to better reflect the candidates' proficiency in meeting the needs of all learners were developed and included. The portfolio is compiled by the end of the pre-clinical internship semester and delivered to the LEA before the clinical internship semester begins.

CLINICAL INTERNSHIP SEMESTER AND TEACHER CERTIFICATION

The clinical internship semester follows the college's sixteen-week semester format. The semester is divided into three main components (see figure 3.2). The first week is spent on campus, with daily six-hour class meetings led by education faculty and clinical supervisors. Activities are focused on preparation for the upcoming semester, communication and collaboration within the cohort, orientation to the internship semester, and content refreshers (e.g., assessment, behavior management, diverse learners, engagement, etc.).

Week one activities are greatly enhanced by the experience and knowledge gained during the pre-clinical internship semester all teacher-candidates engaged in prior. They are able to share specific aspects of their placement within the context of all discussions and activities.

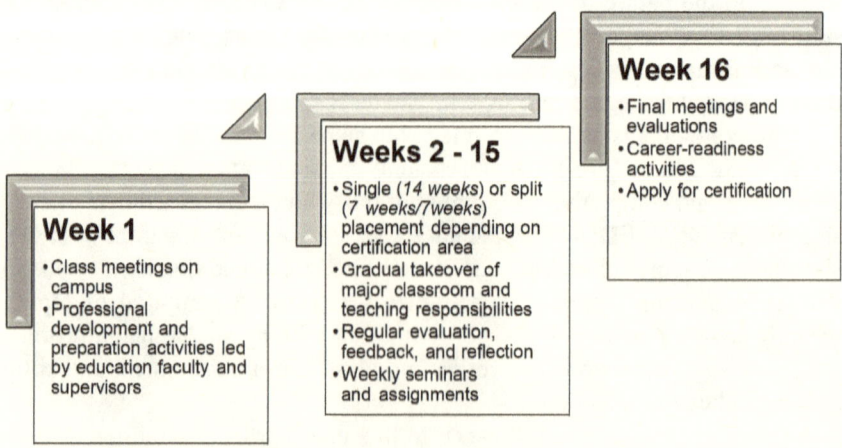

Figure 3.2. Sixteen-week Clinical Internship Semester

Preparation efforts are enriched by the teacher-candidate and supervisor having intimate knowledge of the classroom, mentor-teacher, students, and school district before beginning the fieldwork component in week two. At this point, it is likely any logistical or other concerns have been addressed and everyone is ready to go. In short, the pre-clinical internship semester and thirty hours of fieldwork prior to beginning the internship sets everyone up for a successful experience.

Weeks two through fifteen are spent with the teacher-candidate integrated into the classroom full-time, adhering to the responsibilities and schedule of the LEA. Observations, feedback, and reflection activities occur on a weekly basis, involving the mentor-teacher and supervisor. The authors work with LEAs to incorporate use of video reflection and analysis, in accordance with best reflective practices and the increasing need for a video component to obtain out-of-state certification (e.g., Education Teaching Performance Assessment [edTPA]).

Teacher-candidates meet for a weekly seminar on campus and school-based sites for the duration of the semester. Programming includes guest speakers, career-readiness activities, education technology activities hosted through local stakeholders, and perhaps most importantly, cohort and supervisor discussion, problem-solving, and other supportive activities. Interns are informally observed and evaluated on a regular basis (at minimum every ten days) using a departmental clinical evaluation rubric.

At least two formal evaluation meetings occur during the internship semester (mid-term and final evaluation using the PDE 430 and Lycoming College's Clinical Internship/Professional Semester Evaluation tool) between the mentor-teacher, intern, and supervisor. Mirroring expectations of the education field, high expectations for evidence of growth, as well as proficiency have been established.

Week 16, the college's week of final exams, includes a variety of concluding and celebratory activities. Teacher-candidates work for the entire yearlong modified clinical internship to develop a professional portfolio, detailing their credentials, lesson/unit plans, data analysis experience, and other relevant materials. They then participate in a culminating portfolio exhibition, attended by all members of the college community.

Program faculty work with local stakeholders to develop and implement mock interviews, where teacher-candidates work through a rotation of three to four mock interview sessions with educators and leaders in the community, an activity highly valued by all involved parties. The majority of teacher-candidates will be graduating at this time, and celebrations are planned accordingly. A hallmark of this small, dedicated program is the relationship building that occurs between teacher-candidates, faculty, and staff.

It is amazing to observe teacher-candidates develop from college freshmen to qualified educators ready to enter the field and make a difference. In short, this is what it's all about.

Finally, the chief certification officer conducts hourlong exit interviews with each intern and guides them through the application process for certification. At this point, most teacher-candidates have started the process to obtain employment in the field of education, finding themselves to be competitive and qualified candidates.

I AM MAKING A DIFFERENCE

Lycoming College's teacher preparation program continuously collects and analyzes assessment data based on standards set by PDE and other notable national organizations. Feedback and data from host LEAs are collected on every teacher-candidate (freshman-clinical internship) via Survey Monkey. Data are aggregated and analyzed by education faculty and staff related to dispositions, professionalism, content proficiency, and other important growth indicators. Any notable areas of need are addressed immediately and incorporated into a formal improvement plan, when necessary.

College faculty and staff and LEA administrators submit feedback regarding their perspectives of teacher-candidate readiness, performance, and program effectiveness. Teacher-candidates at all levels complete course evaluations for department and college use. Observation and evaluation forms also contribute and were developed based on Danielson's four domains, Pennsylvania Department of Education (PDE) Field Experience Competencies, and ATE Standards for Field Experiences in Teacher Education. Responses from all involved parties help determine program strengths and needs and serve as a foundation for continuous review and improvement of the program.

Fifty-eight teacher-candidates completed certification programs at Lycoming College over the past three years. Ratings from LEAs compiled during that time demonstrate an average rating out of a possible 3.0 for the following domains:

- 2.86 for Planning and Preparation and Classroom Environment
- 2.6 for Instructional Delivery
- 2.75 for Professionalism

The *Overall* category shows an average of 10.65 of a possible 12.0, with 41 candidates rated *exemplary* and 32 candidates rated *superior*. Also, certification exam pass rates are strong compared across the state (see table 3.1).

Table 3.1. Certification Exam Pass Rates

Year	Lycoming College Pass Rate	Pennsylvania Pass Rate
2017–2018	86%	Not available at this time
2016–2017	93%	77%
2015–2016	83%	75%

Table 3.2. Direct Statements about the Clinical Internship

Role of Individual	Statement
Lycoming Alumni	"When we are able to go out the semester before and observe in the classroom it really helped when it came to student teaching semester because we did not have to waste the first couple weeks going through classroom routines and getting to know the teacher and classroom. We were already knowledgeable on our co-op, the students, and the classroom environments. My co-op even told me that Lycoming is one of the only schools that does this, and she loves the way it works."
Lycoming Alumni	"Biggest strength is the pre-student teaching semester. I loved being able to spend thirty hours in the classroom with my co-op before I started my professional semester."
Mentor-Teacher	"As a secondary mathematics teacher of thirty-one years, I can say I have had many student teachers in my career. I can honestly say that my Lycoming College intern was one of the best student-teachers I have had the privilege of mentoring. Her instructional planning was very evident, as she always arrived prepared for the day's activities. "She willingly gave up her free planning time and even lunch time to help students who required a little additional help or who needed a bit of encouragement. Our students felt as if she genuinely cared about them, both academically and as a person. I definitely felt that her educational training at Lycoming prepared her for her student teaching and she will grow to become a very fine professional teacher, as she is well on her way to becoming an effective teacher."
Student from Another IHE	"It is extremely unfortunate and unprofessional that I don't have the opportunity to meet my placement beforehand. To feel out the classroom and to get to know the teacher, the children, and the curriculum. I literally found out who my mentor-teacher was going to be one week before classes started. I had no time to prepare for living and transportation. It was close enough to my home that I could have commuted, but I had to pay my rent for my campus apartment."

Table 2 includes a small sampling of direct quotes regarding the perspective of success of the modified yearlong clinical internship. Data are consistent with informal communications provided by the vast majority of mentor-teachers. Overwhelming, this is viewed as a beneficial aspect of the program.

In addition to typical course evaluations completed at the end of every course, teacher-candidates take surveys at the end of their program. The survey elicits teacher-candidate satisfaction with the program and effectiveness. These responses are used in tandem with course evaluations and verbal feedback to further determine program strengths and needs.

I AM A MODEL FOR SUCCESS

Lycoming College's teacher preparation program is committed to producing highly effective teacher-candidates who enter the field and have a positive impact on student learning. As evidenced by successful completion of a recent full program review through PDE, the program exceeds accreditation expectations and exemplifies the beliefs of several professional organizations' guiding principles on clinical internships. Data from a variety of sources are utilized to evaluate program effectiveness and make adjustments as appropriate.

Several components of the program contribute to its effectiveness: (a) individual training of mentor-teachers, (b) partner selection for matching teacher-candidates and mentor-teachers, (c) a field placement coordinator, who purposefully places all teacher-candidates from freshmen to senior year of program, (d) trained clinical supervisors, who have a combined forty years of experience in teaching and administration, (e) full-time tenure lined faculty observing and facilitating partnerships with local districts, (f) a teacher handbook that describes program vision, responsibilities, and procedures, (g) individual training of mentor-teachers by clinical supervisors, and (h) individual exit interviews with graduating teacher interns.

While it is acknowledged that many teacher preparation programs implement similar policies and procedures, the authors believe, with data to support as such, a tight and intentional link between the pre-clinical internship semester and clinical internship makes this program distinctive.

REFERENCES

American Association of Colleges for Teacher Education. (2018). *A pivot toward clinical practice, its lexicon, and the renewal of educator preparation: A report of the AACTE Clinical Practice Commission.* Washington, DC: Author.

American Association of Colleges for Teacher Education. (2010). *The clinical preparation of teachers*. Washington, DC: Author.

Association of Teacher Educators (ATE). (2016). ATE–Field Experience Standards. Retrieved from https://ate1.org/field-experience-standards.

Association of Teacher Educators. (2016). *Standards for field experiences in teacher education*. Fairfax, VA: Author.

Clark, A., Triggs, V., & Nielsen, W. (2014). Mentor teacher participation in teacher education: A review of the literature. *Review of Educational Research, 84*(2), 163–202, https://doi: 10.3102/0034654313499618.

Council for the Accreditation of Education Preparation. (2015). Standard 2: Clinical Partnerships and Practice. Retrieved from: http://caepnet.org/standards/standard-2.

Council for Exceptional Children. (2015). *What every special educator must know*. Arlington, VA: Council for Exceptional Children.

Hammerness, K., Darling-Hammond, L., Grossman, P., Rust, F., & Shulman, L. (2005). The design of teacher education programs. In L. Darling-Hammond & J. Bransford (Eds.), *Preparing teachers for a changing world: What teachers should learn and be able to do* (pp. 390–441). San Francisco, CA: Jossey-Bass.

Lycoming College Rankings. (2019). Retrieved from: https://www.usnews.com/best-colleges/lycoming-college-3293/overall-rank.

National Council for Accreditation of Teacher Education. (2010). *Transforming teacher education through clinical practice: A national strategy to prepare effective teachers*. Washington, DC: Blue Ribbon Panel on Clinical Preparation and Partnerships for Improved Student Learning.

Pennsylvania Department of Education. (2011). The Framework for Teaching Evaluation Instrument. Retrieved from: https://static.pdesas.org/content/documents/PDE%20-%20Teacher%20Evaluation%20Pilot%20II%20Rubric.pdf.

Pennsylvania Department of Education. (2012). The Framework for K-12 Program Guidelines. Retrieved from: https://www.education.pa.gov/Documents/Teachers-Administrators/Certification%20Preparation%20Programs/Framework%20Guidelines%20and%20Rubrics/K-12%20Program%20Framework%20Guidelines.pdf.

Chapter Four

Building Relationships and Resilience in a Teacher Residency Program

Strategies for Successful Clinical Experiences

John Lando Carter, EdD; Josh Tipton, EdD; and Ashlee Hover, EdD;
Middle Tennessee State University

The strength of the teacher residency program at Middle Tennessee State University (MTSU) rests upon relationships. Research has consistently shown that positive relationships and interactions between teachers and students can impact student engagement, achievement, and overall educational experience (Hattie, 2012; Pianta, Belsky, Vandergrift, Houts, & Morrison, 2008). Meaningful bonds between teachers and students can simultaneously help students develop stronger achievement behaviors such as increased class participation, self-regulation, and resiliency, while also combating external factors and disengagement that commonly contribute to students' decision to leave school (Henry, Knight, & Thornberry, 2012; Martin, 2014; Meyer & Turner, 2002).

Teacher candidates, like any other students, need the same strong relationships to help them survive the challenges of teacher training and preparation. At MTSU, university faculty work closely with longstanding on-campus and local school district partners to guarantee that all teacher-candidates seeking licensure receive high-quality instruction and are ready to meet the demands of twenty-first-century teaching. However, developing and sustaining these crucial connections takes time and constant reflection upon program sequences, protocols, alignment, and training.

PROGRAM OVERVIEW

In 2010, the educator preparation program at MTSU changed drastically. State mandates from the Tennessee Department of Education first forced the university to adopt a teacher residency model for initial licensure in elementary education, early childhood, middle grades, special education, and secondary education. Second, MTSU was tasked to restart and re-forge partnerships with local and regional school districts. A new dean of education, one with an established level of trust among school leaders and teachers, helped successfully navigate this cultural and programmatic shift to a two-phase residency program staffed by faculty members with proven K–12 teaching and administrative experience.

After struggling to place pre-service teachers, even within local school districts, we now have strong candidate-to-classroom pipelines. Between 2014 and 2018, Rutherford County, which serves as our primary partner district, has hired over two hundred apt and agile MTSU teacher-candidates. Moreover, MTSU has developed resilient ties with more than forty other education agencies [formally recognized by the Tennessee Department of Education], extending our brand beyond the geographic region of middle Tennessee. However, these networks must be sustained and renewed annually to ensure that the MTSU Residency program continues to produce high-quality candidates. Figure 1 shows an overview of our program architecture.

Our residency program encompasses two distinct experiences yet tethers them by design to help students see links across the programs, sustain connections between facilitators and mentors, and make smooth transitions between Residency I and II. The program architecture, however, rests upon deep, meaningful relationships between candidates and mentors. Thus, recruiting and retaining high-quality mentors from local districts is paramount to our success and demands constant teaming throughout the program sequence as well as across programs and colleges. Establishing this candidate-mentor trust begins at the admission phase and continues through the Residency II experience and as candidates transition into their own classrooms.

MENTOR RECRUITING AND
BUILDING RELATIONSHIPS

Relationships are fundamental to success in schools. The success of students, as well as early-career educators, relies upon establishing and nurturing positive and supportive relationships that build motivation, self-efficacy, and resilience (Martin, Marsh, McInerney, & Green, 2009; Tait, 2008). Creating

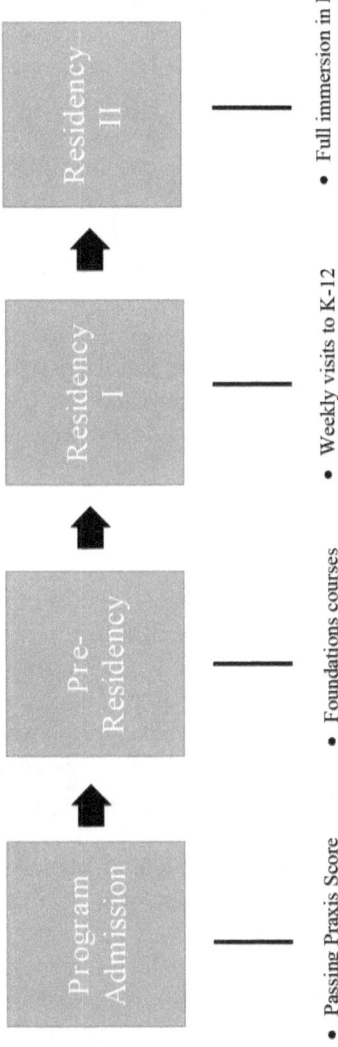

Figure 4.1.

a sense of belonging and connectivity results in the growth of social and emotional skills required to persist in difficult circumstances (De Leon, 2000; Gutman, Sameroff, & Eccles, 2002; Martin et al., 2009; Martin, 2014).

Providing clinical experiences that build both professional expertise and personal growth is critical to the development of highly skilled, confident practitioners who exhibit the level of effectiveness that students and schools deserve. Thus, recruitment of mentors who build appropriate, strong connections with teacher-candidates is a significant aspect of MTSU's residency program.

MTSU education program facilitators recruit and retain exemplary faculty instructors as well as on-site teacher mentors from surrounding school districts and align these team members to specific teacher-candidates' strengths and areas for growth. Potential mentors and field supervisors are selected via a rigorous pre-screening process developed collaboratively between MTSU faculty and school leaders from each of our district partners. For example, the recruitment and selection of Residency II mentors is co-reviewed, revised, and communicated annually and currently demands that mentor teachers have a minimum of four years' teaching experience; further, mentors must be appropriately licensed in alignment with teacher-candidate placement and be rated at a Level of Effectiveness (LOE) of 4 or 5 as determined by the Tennessee Department of Education.

Beginning during their pre-residency coursework, all teacher-candidates are routinely provided with access to experienced and effective mentors. This steady access continues as teacher-candidates progress through their program of study in Residency I, which requires them to be immersed in a pre-K–12 setting each week as well as during Residency II, which is fully field-based and includes student teaching and edTPA (educative teacher performance-assessment) completion. The program sequence and iterative, immersive clinical experiences of the MTSU educator preparation program exposes teacher-candidates to classrooms and quality mentors from start to finish, resulting in more refined and resilient educators who enter the field with preexisting professional and personal relationships.

The significance of relationships is exhibited in MTSU's commitment to collaboration with local education agencies, which requires differentiated approaches to mentor recruitment and retention. For example, teacher-candidates placed in some counties are matched with mentors at the discretion of individual school administrators or liaisons. These local leaders work with university faculty and supervisors to determine mentor selection based upon teacher-candidate need.

In contrast, teacher-candidates placed in other counties or districts are assigned mentors based upon the discretion of district supervisors. In both cases, however, the selection of, and expectations for, mentor-teachers are codified within the mentor-teacher agreements and handbooks provided to each LEA. While MTSU's program must remain agile when navigating the diverse needs of our district partners, the emphasis placed upon upholding high standards for mentor selection, and the development of strong candidate-mentor bonds built upon trust and support, remains essential and is clearly documented within all residency materials disseminated to teacher-candidates, mentors, and district leaders.

The mission and vision for all MTSU mentors and university supervisors emphasizes the relational. For example, the Residency II guidelines used for the selection of mentor-teachers as well as field-experience supervisors establishes the criteria that mentor-teachers and MTSU supervisors exhibit willingness to assume the roles expected of a mentor (e.g., confidante, advocate, coach, and critic). Further, a key responsibility for mentor-teachers outlined in the Residency II handbook is to support the teacher-candidate during the edTPA process by giving emotional support to help the teacher-candidate persist.

Similarly, the responsibilities of MTSU supervisors found within these same resources demands providing advice, assistance, and review for teacher-candidates. The importance placed upon the development of mentor-supervisor-candidate teams is clearly embedded as a central feature of the MTSU residency program and promotes the notion that "good mentors move fluidly among the roles of catalyst, consultant, connector, and collaborator" (Resnick, 2017, p. 112). Thus, relationships are not merely an outcome of teacher-candidates' residency experience; they are an expectation of the university's collaborative agreement with the local education agencies recognized as educator preparation partners.

TALENT MANAGEMENT AND TRANSITIONS

In a large university, providing meaningful learning experiences to all teacher-candidates can be challenging; it requires vertical planning and talent management between pre-residency, Residency I, and Residency II facilitators. Therefore, maintaining and strengthening bonds between university program facilitators, between teacher-candidates and mentor-teachers in the public schools, and between the university and the school partners is vital to the success of preservice teacher training and clinical experiences at MTSU.

When teacher-candidates visit public schools with the right program facilitator at their side and with a carefully selected mentor-teacher, teacher-candidates are primed to experience *flow*, a state of optimal performance where candidates can openly embrace the learning opportunities that intensive fieldwork affords. According to Csikszentmihalyi (2013), the flow state induces an "automatic, effortless, yet highly focused state of consciousness" (p. 110). While in this state, candidates can dismiss anxieties about being novices and leverage the power of learning through failure.

However, this level of vulnerability in learning hinges upon proper alignment between the teacher-candidate, program facilitator, and mentor-teacher in the field. Wagner (2012) reveals how Google, Cisco, and Best Buy not only pursue talent but also put that talent in the right place at the right time. Similarly, MTSU program directors constantly assess and reassess the talent on hand in order to utilize the depth and breadth of knowledge and skills among university faculty and in-field mentors to optimize the residency experience.

For example, Residency I teacher-candidates in the secondary program work together with university facilitators from various K–12 teaching and administrative backgrounds. During the weekly seminar on campus, candidates work within and beyond their discipline with multiple facilitators to receive "just in time" intervention while designing lesson plans or debriefing with each other about in-field experiences (Lezotte & Snyder, 2002, p. 34).

Each facilitator offers background and content skills aligned with students' licensure areas that is immediately accessible to individual candidates. For instance, one residency team consists of four secondary education facilitators with expertise in English language arts, history, technology, and K–12 administration. The facilitators' reservoir of knowledge and experiences provides candidates opportunities not only to discuss best practices but also to understand how to cross-pollinate skills in order to meet the demands of twenty-first-century, interdisciplinary learning.

According to Stronge (2018), "Twenty-first century students need to be able to confront complex ethical questions, engage in productive dialogues across ideological divides, and decide among imperfect options" (p. 119). In order for K–12 students to rise to these new demands, teacher-candidates at MTSU must possess these skills as well.

Modeled after the highly successful practices from the aforesaid businesses, MTSU program facilitators constantly communicate with school partners to ensure that each candidate receives customized coaching throughout their clinical experience, from pre-residency to Residency II. This process is nascent, ongoing, and time intensive, but reciprocal and lasting connections are undoubtedly forged.

USING FIELDWORK TO DEEPEN RELATIONSHIPS

Residency I provides candidates the chance to visit schools weekly for an entire semester with these trained and carefully aligned university facilitators at their sides. At the partner schools, candidates observe teachers, work with teacher mentors, debrief with their university facilitators, experience mini-lessons from administrators, and prepare to teach their own lessons at those same partner schools.

Residency II then allows students to be fully immersed—when possible—in the same partner schools to complete their clinical internship. While student teaching, candidates experience mock job interviews, career fairs, and candid question-and-answer sessions from principals aiming to hire high-quality candidates. As a result, a clinical internship-to-classroom pipeline has been established with many of MTSU's partner districts and schools. In many cases, teacher-candidates work with the same university instructors and teacher mentors across multiple courses and residency experiences to ensure that strong relationships are not only established but also sustained throughout and beyond candidates' clinical experiences.

In Residency II, teacher-candidates complete two placements in public schools. In the first placement, teacher-candidates must submit and pass the edTPA to demonstrate their abilities to plan, instruct, and assess students in the classroom. Teacher-candidates design a learning segment of three to five lessons for edTPA at the beginning of the first placement, which can be overwhelming for many teacher-candidates. For example, one former teacher-candidate explained, *"It would be more beneficial to have some experience with teaching every day in a classroom and having to come up with lesson plans on a daily basis before being required to also participate in edTPA."* Throughout the teacher preparation program, students value the time with their mentor-teachers in the public schools and desire more time in the classroom with them through co-teaching experiences.

A short turnaround between starting Residency II in a new school placement with a different mentor-teacher and beginning the edTPA demanded a programmatic change. Thus, our early childhood program facilitators decided to assign their teacher-candidates to the same mentor-teacher for both Residency I and II. Since then, other programs within the college of education have leveraged the relational benefits of this trend as well.

For example, the transition from Residency I to II with the same mentors for math and science secondary education students grew from the university Residency I facilitators hosting an on-site meeting with potential Residency I mentor-teachers at one of the local high schools. The university facilitator explained to the potential mentors that if the connections between the Residency I students and teacher-mentors resulted in strong, mutually benefiting relationships, then Residency II placements could also be assigned for the same classroom. This has helped not only stabilize but also strengthen the program in two high need content areas—math and science.

After Residency I, the university facilitator reached out to both the teacher-candidates and the mentor-teachers separately to ask whether they wanted to pursue the same placement in Residency II. Thus far, all math and science mentor-teachers have requested that the Residency I students return to their classrooms for Residency II. In fact, we have begun conducting on-site edTPA seminars for the teacher-candidates at the local high school, and mentor-teachers have requested to be more involved with this process.

Teacher-candidates who completed Residency I and II in the same placement have reported that they feel more comfortable with the edTPA expectations and process of submission during Residency II because they have established networks comprised of mentor-teachers, school faculty, school administration, and the students from their Residency I placements. A key component of the edTPA is the *context for learning* that requires candidates to collect data about the students in the class they teach.

When teacher-candidates are allowed to transition from Residency I to Residency II with the same classroom placements, they report that they have more time to correctly identify the students' diverse learning needs and to accommodate and modify lesson plans for specific types of students including special education students and English Language Learners. In addition, teacher-candidates have more time to identify the diverse cultural, personal, and community assets that students bring to the school and classroom environment.

Furthermore, school administrators have expressed an interest in maintaining consistent Residency I and Residency II placements, which allows them to observe teacher-candidates' abilities and potentially identify future faculty members. The procedures that the early childhood, math secondary, and science secondary program facilitators have undertaken to transition teacher-candidates from Residency I to Residency II with the same mentor-teachers have become models for future programs at MTSU.

SUSTAINING STRONG MENTOR RELATIONSHIPS THROUGH ITERATIVE COLLABORATION AND TRAINING

Aligning talent and using fieldwork as a way to deepen relationships requires ongoing training and professional development in order to enhance the university facilitators' and teacher-mentors' skills. Debriefing sessions, boot camp events, and data retreats demand that the stakeholders involved in training teacher-candidates at MTSU commit to a mission of continuous improvement in their own knowledge and skills. Just like the teacher-candidates, they learn, unlearn, and relearn in order to develop and sustain connections that extend beyond Residency II.

Debriefing sessions for secondary Residency I program facilitators began as biannual meetings to reflect upon the outcomes of the current semester. These debriefing sessions were initially logistically focused but soon were aimed at answering the following reflective questions:

What went well?
What could have gone better?
What might we need to learn/practice to do better next time?
(Brown, Roediger, & McDaniel, 2014, p. 155)

The focus on relationships emerged naturally out of this reflective practice and also changed the frequency of the debriefing sessions from once after each semester to once per month during the semester as well. This shift in focus and frequency helped uncover what was working and what was needing strengthening regarding students' bonds with program facilitators, in-field mentors, and each other.

Similarly, Residency I Boot Camps began as intensive pre-planning sessions for the upcoming fall or spring semesters. Although these sessions were vital, several key groups were not present. The boot camp has now become an all-inclusive daylong event that is the bedrock for building reciprocal relationships in the MTSU Residency program. Program facilitators plan meet-and-greets, arrange keynote speeches from our surrounding district partners, and hold question-and-answer sessions where teacher-candidates often ask about classroom management concerns or issues in work-life balance. A highlight always comes from visiting administrators, who will soon be seeing these candidates walking their own hallways, answer questions freely and candidly. This event establishes the root of the residency relationships through openness and vulnerability. Program facilitators actively solicit feedback from in-field mentors, administrators, and the teacher-candidates themselves to ensure that candidates know that all stakeholders involved share the same student success mission.

The Annual Data Retreat, which is the newest addition to our training protocol, spans beyond the residency teams and calls upon the entire college of education to reflect, recalibrate, and share strategies across programs in the college. The teams participate in roundtable discussions, data chats, and accreditation debriefs during this event. The data retreat is a powerful opportunity for program facilitators and local district partners to share ideas, analyze edTPA data, and continue to search for ways to enhance the effectiveness of the many unique yet interlocking licensure programs at MTSU.

CONCLUSION

After nearly a decade of trial and error, the residency program at MTSU has moved from struggling to place pre-service teachers to developing pipelines to the classroom for strong teacher-candidates. Steady relationship-building has taken MTSU beyond just the mid-state area with partnerships now in over forty local education agencies. At a time when educators are leaving the profession at the highest rate on record (Hackman & Morath, 2018) and student enrollment in many teacher preparation programs continues to decline, EPPs must realign residency and clinical experiences to leverage the power of relationships to ensure long-term student success, both for teacher-candidates and their future pupils. However, this is no singular endeavor. According to Coyle (2018), "a mere hint of belonging is not enough" (p. 12). It is rather a perennial renewing of relationships for all stakeholders involved that will provide the next generation of teachers with the resilience they need to survive and thrive in the twenty-first-century classroom.

REFERENCES

Brown, P. C., Roediger, H. L., & McDaniel, M. A. (2014). *Make it stick: The science of successful learning.* Cambridge, MA: Harvard University Press.

Coyle, D. (2018). *The culture code: Secrets of highly successful groups.* New York: NY: Bantam.

Csikszentmihalyi, M. (2013). *Creativity: Flow and the psychology of discovery and invention.* New York, NY: Harper Perennial.

De Leon, G. (2000). *The therapeutic community: Theory, model and method.* New York, NY: Springer Publishing Company.

Gutman, L. M., Sameroff, A., & Eccles, J. S. (2002). The academic achievement of African American students during early adolescents: An examination of multiple risk, promotive, and protective factors. *American Journal of Community Psychology, 30,* 401–28.

Hackman, M., & Morath, E. (December 28, 2018). Teachers quit jobs at highest rate on record. *Wall Street Journal.* Retrieved from https://www.wsj.com/articles/teachers-quit-jobs-at-highest-rate-on-record-11545993052.

Hattie, J. (2012). *Visible learning for teachers: Maximizing impact on learning.* New York, NY: Routledge.

Henry, K. L., Knight, K. E., & Thornberry, T. P. (2012). School disengagement as a predictor of dropout, delinquency, and problem substance use during adolescence and early adulthood. *Journal of Youth and Adolescence, 41*(2), 156–66.

Lezotte, L. W., & Snyder, K. M. (2002). *Assembly required: A continuous school improvement system.* Okemos, MI: Effective Schools Products.

Martin, A. (2014). Interpersonal relationships and students' academic and non-academic development. In D. Zandvliet, P. den Brok, T. Mainhard, & J. van Tartwijk (Eds.), *Interpersonal relationships in education: From theory to practice* (pp. 9–24). Rotterdam, Netherlands: Sense Publishers.

Martin, A. J., Marsh, H. W., McInerney, D. M., & Green, J. (2009). Young people's interpersonal relationships and academic and non-academic outcomes: The relative salience of teachers, parents, same-sex peers, and opposite-sex peers. *Teachers College Record*, March, http://www.tcrecord.org.

Meyer, D. K., & Turner, J. C. (2002). Discovering emotion in classroom motivation research. *Educational Psychologist, 37*, 107–14.

Pianta, R. C., Belsky, J., Vandergrift, N., Houts, R., & Morrison, F. J. (2008). Classroom effects on children's achievement trajectories in elementary school. *American Educational Research Journal, 45*(2), 365–97.

Resnick, M. (2017). *Lifelong kindergarten: Cultivating creativity through projects, passion, peers, and play*. Cambridge, MA: The MIT Press.

Stronge, J. (2018). *Qualities of effective teachers*. Alexandria, VA: ASCD.

Tait, M. (2008). Resilience as a contributor to novice teacher success, commitment, and retention. *Teacher Education Quarterly, 35*(4), 57–75.

Wagner, T. (2012). *Creating innovators: The making of young people who will change the world*. New York, NY: Scribner.

Chapter Five

Empowering All Voices

Meaningful Mentoring Designed for a University-School Partnership

Christopher Clinton, EdD, and Maureen P. Hall, PhD, University of Massachusetts Dartmouth

Interpersonal relationships are at the center of all teaching and learning. Effective mentoring is the glue that makes these relationships positive and generative—serving to improve learning on all levels. There are many relationships inherent in any schooling, and the relationships between and among students, teachers, parents, administrators, and community members must be cultivated and maintained.

The work in this chapter documents an ongoing project between a public university in the Northeast and a local urban school district. The work of this project aligns with the main theme of the American Educational Research Association (AERA) for 2020; that theme is "The Power and Possibilities for the Public Good When Researchers and Organizational Stakeholders Collaborate." While the AERA theme draws upon the disconnect between researchers and organizational stakeholders, this chapter focuses on a collaboration with mentoring at the center; it is the glue that connects students, teachers, university professors, and administrators in generative ways.

Collegiality is the foundation to building a culture of change (Allen, 2009; Brouwer & Korthagen, 2005). Mentoring and induction for teacher-candidates provide not only for the traditional exchange of ideas and the spread of effective pedagogies, but most importantly, they provide an opportunity to create a social dynamic through which professional relationships can be built.

Professional, interpersonal dynamics, once woven into the school culture through the use of mentoring, is intended to support partner school stakeholders as they overcome the uncertainty of their daily work. Moreover, in an urban environment, it is these professional relationships that best support both perseverance and retention while encouraging the development of pedagogical strategies in new teacher practitioners. Professional collegiality becomes emblematized as a critical element in building a positive school culture (Deal & Peterson, 2016).

CHALLENGES OF THE TEACHING PROFESSION

Effective mentoring can shield and support teacher-candidates from some of the more toxic elements of the school culture, ones that isolate and disconnect stakeholders from the larger school community. Mentoring provides the needed development and support for generative relationships. In turn, these supports create a support network focused on individual well-being and professional growth of educators.

The mentoring model illustrated in this chapter centers on mentoring as an effective way of addressing several challenges faced by a large urban school district and a local university located in the northeast United States. The first and most readily identifiable problem in the school district is one of retention. The local urban school district has approximately 850 teachers. For the last three years, between 23 percent and 26 percent of those teachers have either moved to other districts or left the profession. This turnover of more than two hundred teachers per year has created a "barbell effect" between veteran teachers and new hires.

The barbell analogy illustrates a state of a high turnover district where there are many teachers in a district are new and have three years or less experience and only veteran teachers with ten years or more teaching experience remain. There is a gap of experience between them. "Urban schools have teachers with lesser qualifications" (Lankford, Loeb, & Wyckoff, 2002, p. 44), and almost half of new hires leave urban schools within five years (Henke, Chen, & Geis, 2000; Ingersoll, 2003). As Ingersoll (2004) concludes, unequal access to experienced and highly qualified teachers is "a major factor in the stratification of educational opportunity" (p. 4). The retained veteran teachers have an additional substantial burden placed upon them to maintain current education targets and (where possible) improve the school and district in the revolving door of teacher retention.

The second challenge involves the ongoing changes in the guidelines and regulations at the state level. The Massachusetts Department of Elementary and Secondary Education initiated new teacher preparation program (TPP) guidelines where universities were tasked to develop specific gateway assessments for teacher-candidates. These gateway assessments are intended to "define minimum performance standards that candidates must meet in order to pass the assessment and ultimately advance beyond the pre-practicum" (MA Dept of Education website, 2018). The opportunity to provide authentic experiences in the teacher-candidate context and scaffold these early field-based experiences create an opportunity to support a stronger connection between the TPP and the K–12 school partner.

The final challenge identified was the disconnect between the TPP at the local university and the hiring district. The public perception of the university as an "ivory tower," and its implied detachment from society has fallen out of favor and has been replaced with the mandate to produce generations of more skilled labor (Scott, 2005). The lack of voice by the K–12 partners in the TPP and its effectiveness in preparing urban educators was also addressed through this mentoring model. From the point of view of the University's TPP, this challenge presents an opportunity for the TPP to design a new program to specifically target the needs of this urban district.

THEORETICAL FRAMEWORK

At least two different yet connected theoretical perspectives provide an underpinning for this work. These are Social Interdependence Theory (SIT) and Social Emotional Learning (SEL).

Social Interdependence Theory

One of the theoretical perspectives relevant to this chapter is closely related to Morton and Deutsch's social interdependence theory (Deutsch, 1949). Social interdependence, the basis of cooperative learning, is a theory describing how individuals are affected by one another's actions. For example, social interdependence is present when the goal achievement of a particular individual influences the goal achievement of another (Johnson & Johnson, 2005).

The establishment of this mentoring model is designed to connect the goals of the TPP at the university with their K–12 partner school districts. The dynamics of these groups, both grounded in their support for optimal teacher preparation, have an alignment of goals that are best supported in a cooperative, socially interdependent environment. This dynamic environment determines the success or failure of their shared goal of an improved educational culture.

Social Emotional Learning

The second theory underpinning this project is Social Emotional Learning (SEL), which is the process through which children and adults acquire and effectively apply the knowledge, attitudes, and skills necessary to understand and manage emotions, set and achieve positive goals, feel and show empathy for others, establish and maintain positive relationships, and make responsible decisions (CASEL, 2019).

Substantial evidence exists indicating that cooperative efforts cultivate the following: a greater determination to achieve the shared goals, stronger organizational relationships, and improved psychological health of the participants participating in the mentoring program (Johnson & Johnson, 2005). Social interdependence is present when the actions of the individuals participating in the mentoring program affect the shared outcomes of veteran mentor-teachers and teacher-candidates. Those with positive goal interdependence and supportive positive professional relationships gain higher achievement than those who work alone and have few opportunities to interact with others (Johnson & Johnson, 2005).

Efforts to improve education through mentoring often focus only on instructional and curricular issues and overlook the social and emotional dimensions of teaching and learning—critical to teacher and teacher-candidate success. However, as Parker Palmer (1998) points out, "Educational institutions are full of divisive structures" (p. 36); these structures often distance students and teachers. Social Emotional Learning (SEL) serves as a remedy for this division, providing a systematic framework of skills that can be a used for the creation of positive mentor-teacher and student-teacher relationships inside and outside the classroom.

THE TEACHER MENTORING MODEL

Phase 1—Recruitment

The initial outreach began with the districts' mentoring coordinator reaching out to building principals to identify their exemplary veteran teachers. During this phase, the university worked to establish a free-of-charge, three-credit mentoring course for up to twenty employees of the district. This would be the first time the university provided a free course to students. The university was incentivized to offer this course as the education department planned on recruiting these veteran educators taking this course to become the mentor-teachers. These veteran teachers would then be hired by the TPP to become mentor-teachers who will then be tasked to share their classrooms and experience in the development and support teacher-candidates.

The course was designed to be taught at the district's high school for fourteen weeks for four hours per week. The term "host teacher" was also adopted by the TPP to better align with language from the states' Elementary and Secondary Department of Education. The TPP established three zero-credit courses for field-based experiences (FBE) to have gateway assessments. Finally, during this phase, a plan was sent to the university provost to establish a field experiences "fee" (replacing other university fees), which was to be dispersed to the host teachers upon completion of the FBE.

Phase 2—Mentoring Course

The course opens with the mentor-teachers defining the skills and dispositions of a successful educator in their district. The assignment asked the veteran educators to indicate where and when the teacher-candidate was to introduce, practice, and then demonstrate these essential skills and dispositions. Weekly, the veteran mentor-teachers were asked using polling software their opinions on issues of teacher-candidate development. After defining critical skills for new teachers, the veteran mentor-teachers were asked, "When do teacher-candidates get to practice these skills?"

Many of the veteran mentor-teachers did not see a real time to "practice" until after they were hired by the district. Moreover, they all believed in a "mutual respect" classroom environment made for a much higher likelihood of success with more challenging populations of students. Another success oriented essential skill they included was they believed in-service teachers should know how to balance the engagement factor versus the depth of content. When practitioners were asked, "At what point do you see teacher-candidates being capable of demonstrating these skills?," most said not until between five and seven years after full-time employment.

As part of the course curriculum, the veteran mentor-teachers identified the challenges and the depth of "practice" necessary to develop new teachers. It was at this phase the veteran mentor-teachers started to think critically on how the university TPP could provide experiences and coursework supportive to the specific needs identified by this urban district. One of the specific tasks assigned to the veteran mentor-teachers was the creation of an event calendar where the veteran mentor-teachers identified key times during the year when teacher-candidates were most likely to observe and participate in meaningful activities in schools and classrooms. In addition, the mentoring course reexamined the district's own induction program with the goal to align where and when essential skills and dispositions were being reinforced during the school year.

The mentoring course went onto train the veteran teachers in the states' Candidate Assessment of Performance (CAP) teacher practicum evaluation tool. This tool is the states' replacement for the teacher performance assessment (EdTPA). The most significant difference between the CAP and EdTPA is that the CAP uses six elements of the states' unified Educator Evaluation system to measure the readiness of teacher-candidates prior to attaining initial licensure. The measure of the six elements of the CAP is the same measure used by professional teachers (DESE, 2017). This training was instructive to the veteran mentor-teachers/host-teachers, as it involved a good deal of calibration training. More importantly, the mentor-teachers were trained on how to quickly identify high-quality evidence of instruction and then how to give meaningful/mindful feedback to teacher-candidates.

This activity supported the teacher-candidates as it provided concrete guidance on how they were to be measured as effective educators once hired by the district. Because measuring teacher readiness and effectiveness is a difficult task for even the most veteran mentor-teacher, the course introduced David Rock's SCARF model (Rock, 2008) on influencing behavior by constructively giving feedback. The integration of this model had a substantive impact on how the mentor-teachers perceived their interactions with their mentees.

David Rock's SCARF model is grounded in neuroscience and made up of five domains. These domains create the acronym SCARF and stand for: Status, Certainty, Autonomy, Relatedness, and Fairness. When implemented in a positive fashion, these five domains activate the same neurological reward circuitry that physical rewards may activate, like money. When implemented poorly, they activate the same neurological threat circuitry of physical threats, like pain (Rock, 2008). When applied to education, we adapt the model to give feedback to teacher-candidates thinking about the teacher-candidates' SEL in relation to the five domains:

1. Status, and the teacher-candidates' perception and relative importance to others.
2. Certainty, addressing the teacher-candidates' concerns about being able to predict the future.
3. Autonomy, providing the teacher-candidates with a sense of control over classroom events.
4. Relatedness, developing the sense of safety between mentor and teacher-candidate.
5. Fairness, and the teacher-candidates' perception of fair exchanges in the feedback.

The SCARF model is an easy way to remember and act upon the social triggers that can generate both the approach and avoid responses. The goal of this model is to help minimize the easily activated threat responses and maximize positive engaged states of mind during attempts to collaborate with and influence others. As a model, it focuses on SEL and promotes positive social interdependence improving relationships between veteran mentor-teachers and teacher-candidates.

Phase 3—Integration

The inclusion of the practitioner voice in the TPP with a lens focusing on mentoring and preparing teachers to be effective in an urban environment was the goal of this mentoring program. As mentioned in the introduction, this work aligns with the AERA 2020 theme connecting researchers and organizational stakeholders democratically. Essentially, all members of a collaborative group are granted equal footing and the space is "democratized." All voices are listened to and respected.

The first point of integration was the construction of three gateway assessments (see appendix A) designed by the veteran mentor-teachers. These assessments were developed into zero credit courses by the TPP and integrated into field-based experiences. This new model allows a mentor-teacher to provide both the classroom/field-based experience and provide the critical feedback to teacher-candidates by means of these the gateway assessments.

The first semester assessment includes a case study of an instructional issue as defined by the host teacher. In the second semester the assignment includes the delivery of a classroom lesson or unit designed to show student growth between a pre- and a post-assessment. The third semester assessment asks the teacher-candidate to produce and deliver a unit of lessons that demonstrates a variety of teaching strategies, focuses on differentiated instruction, and collects and measures evidence of student learning.

The second point of integration was a crosswalk document that outlined the University courses, the essential questions, and the habits and skills linking the coursework to gateway assessments. This document provides guidance to university faculty to better inform the course objectives for the selective syllabi so the coursework may better align toward scaffolding the field-based experiences while remaining separate from those experiences.

The final point of integration was from the university leadership. The university provided a means for the mentor-teachers to invoice the TPP to be able to be paid to provide feedback on the gateway assessments. The payment of $150 is given to the mentor-teacher to provide critical feedback on each gateway assessment. This critical feedback informs the TPP on the teacher-candidate's progress in field-based experience portion of the program. If they do not produce a satisfactory portfolio of work as measured by both the veteran mentor-teacher and the TPP, the teacher-candidate will be asked to repeat the field-based experience through the zero-credit course. The teacher-candidate will then be offered the choice to remain with this mentor-teacher or choose another possible placement from those mentor-teachers who are identified as mentors by the district and have taken the university course. The TPP has also asked for two host teachers to participate on the Teacher Education Advisory Committee, whose mandate is to evaluate the K–12 partnership and to make suggestions to the TPP for practical changes to the field-based experiences.

INSIGHTS

In the past, although practitioners have done the work of teaching and learning—developing standards, providing placements, and even giving meaningful feedback to teacher-candidates at the end of their preservice experience—the voice and role of the practitioner has been largely underutilized and undervalued in university TPPs. Moreover, as Bernhardt and Koester (2015) underline, host teachers don't always get the "necessary training and support to guide their work with pre-service teachers" (p. 37).

This work evidences how training and valuing the practitioner voice is vital to TPPs and should be an obvious extension of all teacher preparation programs. The work represents this shift, and this mentoring model showcases the myriad opportunities for all stakeholders in teacher preparation programs. For example, teacher-candidates in the mentoring model are given greater opportunities to "practice" teaching techniques and receive critical feedback from practitioners. Field-based experiences are made more relevant and impactful through a more developed and intensive mentoring model. In addition, host teachers begin to recognize the value of mentoring, which also shapes school culture in positive ways and builds more meaningful professional relationships.

One of the most impactful opportunities identified by the veteran mentor-teachers, when given a short three-question qualitative end-of-course survey, was the insight they gained when asked to think critically about what skills and dispositions the district identified in them to be chosen as mentor-teachers. Nearly all of the veteran mentor-teachers found the process of reflection on what skills and dispositions made them successful and how challenging it would be to expect teacher-candidates to demonstrate these same skills and dispositions. In a second question, the mentor-teachers were asked what they valued being "passed down" to the teacher-candidates. One mentor-teacher in the program shared this reflection on how this mentor model underlined the positive relationship-building:

> I really enjoyed thinking about how important it was to have a strong connection to the person you're working with. . . . So I guess the social emotional piece I've never really considered being as important as the "here is how to take attendance" piece. I really had to think about what skills I need when working with young adults and not just students. (middle school mentor-teacher 1, personal communication, December 12, 2018)

Another positive insight from the veteran mentor-teachers was their ability to give feedback to the student teachers. They knew they would have several semesters to observe these teacher-candidates develop. This aligned with their knowledge that developing into a teaching professional takes time. Having more time allowed for more trusting professional relationships to evolve, and giving feedback became more effective. Teacher-candidates could reflect and adjust their teaching in response to quality feedback.

An elementary-school veteran mentor-teacher shared similar reflections. She believed getting to know a teacher-candidate over several semesters would help to develop relationships with them and was practical in order to provide the time and contact necessary for the development of the teacher-candidate. This mentor-teacher also made connections for how quality mentoring might influence or affect the possible hiring of these teacher-candidates in the future. She expounded:

> I foresee this being significant when it comes time to hiring and having the student who you've known the strengths and weaknesses of at the hiring table, it should make it really easy for the principal at that point. (elementary school mentor-teacher 1, personal communication, December 12, 2018)

Many of the mentor-teachers saw the additional benefits of being able to give feedback and input to teacher-candidates. Another participant, a high school veteran mentor-teacher, also reflected on the sustainability of this mentoring model and possible connections to future employment:

> It is very much like an apprentice program and because I know the student teachers better, I feel as though I can have some of the more difficult conversations about what they might need to improve upon. This will make their first year as the new hire more successful! (high school veteran mentor-teacher 1, personal communication, December 12, 2018)

From the K–12 partner district's point of view, this new mentoring model has met or exceeded expectations. The high school principal also shared this:

> The only question I have to ask to the mentor teacher is, "If I hired them would you continue to be their induction coordinator?" If the answer is yes, then I know it's likely to be a good fit for the department. (high school principal, personal communication, December 3, 2018)

Further evidence of the effectiveness of this mentor model is, at the date of publication, 100 percent of the teacher-candidates who applied to the district have been employed by the district and are being inducted by their clinical experience mentor-teacher.

DISCUSSION

The best teaching and learning involves the development of strong relationships and attention to the social and emotional dimensions of what it means to be human. Overall, the mentoring program more deeply integrates with the teacher-candidate experience, and, in doing so, more readily supports the social dynamic through which positive school cultures are supported. The program elements of identifying what works in the district, defining what is expected and scaffolded in the teacher candidate's FBE, providing feedback, and being remunerated for feedback on gateway assessments are critical to the overall program success.

Shifting the scope of time from multiple host teachers and a variety of locations for the FBE to a more targeted model of preparing teacher-candidates for a single urban environment with a single veteran mentor-teacher allows the mentoring program to "go deep, not wide" in its allocation of time and resources. Measuring success of the mentoring program by the measures of hiring (in a targeted urban district) and overall retention (in that same district) allows the university–K–12 partnership to address the "barbell" of human resources currently observed in the district.

This mentoring program provides another significant pathway for host teachers to change a school culture through promotive interactions and developing SEL skills in new hires. The model has similarities with the model set forth by Sanchez et al. (2016), as they make clear that training is needed for the mentor-teachers. They put forth the term "educative mentoring," and argue, "we must reconceptualize the role of cooperating teachers as field-based teacher educators and provide the professional development and support necessary for this role" (p. 71).

Likewise, in the mentoring model, the host teachers' voices are valued as they actively develop new inductees to the district and, in essence, prepare teacher-candidates for future roles in the district. A community is created and maintained, and as Deal and Peterson point out, "Thriving school cultures are knit together with community ideals using local resources and shaped in accordance with community ideals and expectations" (2016, p. 145). Although school leadership provides an overarching frame for the community "tapestry," in the mentoring model put forth in this chapter, host teachers provide the quality of the thread.

The incorporation of practitioner "voice" early in the mentoring of teacher-candidates not only allows for greater classroom opportunities and the development of pedagogical practices, but it highlights the need to focus on the development of social-emotional learning as the cornerstone for building positive social interdependence. This model demonstrates if the mentoring relationship is focused, meaningful, and given the time to develop the university and K–12 partnership can provide a means of addressing many current challenges in urban schools. In addition, this model adds one more puzzle piece to the literature in terms of how universities and schools can work in unison to improve teacher preparation programs.

APPENDIX A: FIELD-BASED EXPERIENCES FIELDWORK

FIELD-BASED EXPERIENCES 1—EDU 536
(Co-Registration with EDU 511/521)

- Observation log
- Case study of the classroom/school using classroom data
- Identification of challenge in the classroom
- Completed interview with host teacher on developing Student Learning Goals
- Engagement in small group tutoring, individual student support
- Evaluation of Gateway Assignment (completed by host teacher)
- Disposition survey (completed by teacher/administrator at school site)
- Host Teacher Survey (completed by student)

FIELD-BASED EXPERIENCES 2—EDU 537
(Co-Reg. with EDU 512/522)

- Observation log
- Completion of two Lesson Plans

- Completion of one Formative and one Summative Assessment
- Design, execution, and evaluation of a Formative Assessment
- Co-planning and co-teaching of (at least) one Whole Group Lesson
- Delivery of individual instruction to whole class
- Design, execution, and evaluation of a Summative Assessment
- Reflections post-delivery of each lesson and assessment
- Evaluation of Gateway Assignment (completed by host teacher)
- Disposition survey (completed by teacher/administrator at school site)
- Host Teacher Survey (completed by student)

FIELD-BASED EXPERIENCES PART 3—EDU 538
(Co-Reg. with EDU 552/602)

- Observation log
- Co-planning and co-teaching of an independent A Unit of no less than five lessons
- Design Unit Plan Highlighting SEI strategies and student outcomes
- Design, execution, and evaluation of Formative and Summative Assessments
- Reflections post-delivery of each lesson and assessment
- Evaluation of Gateway Assignment (completed by host teacher)
- Dispositions survey (completed by teacher/administrator at school site)
- Host Teacher Survey (completed by student)

NOTE: Completion of Field-Based Experiences is extended throughout the academic school year. However, you may not enter your next phase of Field-Based Experiences until you have passed the course and completed the hours for the previous phase.

REFERENCES

Allen, J. M. (2009). Valuing practice over theory: How beginning teachers re-orient their practice in the transition from the university to the workplace. *Teaching and Teacher Education, 25*(5), 647–54.

Bernhardt, P., & Koester, M. (2015). Preparing mentors: Professional development to support clinical practice. *The Field Experience Journal, 15*(1), 37–57.

Brackett, M. A., & Rivers, S. E. (2014). Transforming students' lives with social and emotional learning. *International Handbook of Emotions in Education, 1–22.* Retrieved from http://casel.org/research/sel-in-your-state/.

Brouwer, N., & Korthagen, F. (2005). Can teacher education make a difference? *American Educational Research Journal, 42*(1), 153–224.

Cook-Sather, A. (2014). Student-faculty partnership in explorations of pedagogical practice: A threshold concept in academic development. *International Journal for Academic Development, 19*(3), 186–98.

Deal, T. E., & Peterson, K. D. (2016). *Shaping school culture.* Hoboken, NJ, USA: John Wiley & Sons, Inc. https://doi.org/10.1002/9781119210214.

Department of Elementary & Secondary Education (2017). *CAP Guidelines—Educator Preparation.* (n.d.). Retrieved from http://www.doe.mass.edu/edprep/cap/guidelines.html.

Department of Elementary & Secondary Education (2018). *Guidelines—educator preparation resources educator preparation.* Retrieved from http://www.doe.mass.edu/edprep/resources/guidelines.html.

Johnson, D. W., & Johnson, R. T. (2005). New developments in social interdependence theory. *Genetic, Social, and General Psychology Monographs, 131*(4), 285–358.

Henke, R., Chen, X., & Geis, S. (2000). *Progress through the teacher pipeline: 1992–1993 college graduates and elementary/secondary school teaching as of 1997* (Paper No. NCES 20000152). Washington, DC: National Center for Education Statistics.

Ingersoll, R. (2003). *Is there really a teacher shortage? Philadelphia, PA: Consortium for Policy Research in Education, University of Pennsylvania.* Retrieved from http://www.gse.upenn.edu/pdf/rmi/Shortage-RMI-09-2003.pdf.

Ingersoll, R. M. (2004). *Why do high-poverty schools have difficulty staffing their classrooms with qualified teachers?* Washington, DC: Center for American Progress.

Lankford, H., Loeb, S., & Wyckoff, J. (2002). Teacher sorting and the plight of urban schools: A descriptive analysis. *Educational Evaluation and Policy Analysis, 24*(1), 37–62.

Deutsch, M. (1949). A Theory of Co-operation and Competition. *Human Relations. 2*(2), 129–52. https://doi.org/10.1177/001872674900200204.

Owen-Smith, P. (2004). What is cognitive-affective learning? *Journal of Cognitive Affective Learning,* 1(1), 11.

Palmer, P. J. (1998) *The courage to teach: Exploring the landscape of a teacher's life.* San Francisco, CA: Wiley.

Rock, D. (2008). SCARF: A brain-based model for collaborating with and influencing others. *NeuroLeadership Journal, 1*(1), 44–52.

Salovey, P., & Mayer, J. D. (1990). Emotional intelligence. *Imagination, Cognition and Personality, 9*(3), 185–211.

Sanchez, S. R., Roegman, R., & Goodwin, A. L. (2016). The multiple roles of mentors. *Phi Delta Kappan, 98*(2), 66–71.

Schonert-Reichl, K. A. (2017). Social and emotional learning and teachers. *Future of Children, 27*(1), 137–55. https://doi.org/10.1353/foc.2017.0007.

Waxler, R. P., & Hall, M.P. (2011). *Transforming literacy: Changing lives through reading and writing.* Bingley, England: Emerald Insight Publishing.

Chapter Six

Mentoring the Mentors
Developing Culturally Efficacious Educators within a Residency Model

Jennifer Gilardi Swoyer, PhD; Lorena Claeys, PhD;
Belinda Bustos Flores, PhD;
Claudia Treviño García, PhD; Lucinda Juárez, PhD;
Lisa Santillán, PhD; Lucinda N. Sohn, PhD;
The University of Texas at San Antonio

Mentor-teachers are traditionally positioned as the experts who guide teacher-candidates from an initial apprenticeship phase to becoming full participants in the professional community (Gardiner, 2011; Reinhardt, 2017). There is often an assumption that mentors intuitively have the knowledge and skills to support teachers through these developmental stages, and that it is only the teacher-candidate who is transformed through the process (Flores, Gist, & Claeys, 2018).

However, for successful growth to be cultivated, both the mentor-teacher and the teacher-candidate must be open to the process of critical reflection on their individual and shared practices. This chapter provides an overview of how a four-year public Hispanic Serving Institution (HSI) is transforming their educator preparation program (EPP) to provide space for continuous professional learning on culturally efficacious practices (CEP) for teacher-candidates, mentor-teachers, and university faculty through the Teacher Residency Model 2.0 (TRM 2.0).

In regard to metacognitive mentoring practices, we specifically address how participating in a Culturally Efficacious Professional Learning Community (CE-PLC) and reflecting on our developmental experiences of becoming culturally efficacious mentors while mentoring others is helping guide the university's transformation of its EPP.

This chapter includes five sections: (1) mentoring opportunities and challenges within the initial stages of developing and implementing the TRM 2.0, (2) a description of the theoretical framework guiding the culturally efficacious lens for mentoring and instructional practices, (3) an overview of the TRM 2.0, (4) lessons learned about preparing culturally efficacious mentor-teachers through a yearlong residency model, and (5) implications and suggestions for EPPs to support mentor-teachers and university-based educators on their journey of becoming culturally efficacious mentors.

MENTORING OPPORTUNITIES AND CHALLENGES WITHIN THE TEACHER RESIDENCY MODEL 2.0

The goal of the TRM 2.0 is to prepare educators with the knowledge, skills, professional experience, and cultural awareness necessary to meet the needs of our rapidly expanding ethnically, linguistically, and racially diverse student populations. The clinical aspect of the TRM 2.0 built on the traditional EPP by extending concentrated mentor-led time in the field from a semester to a yearlong experience.

Conceivably, the extended time provides more opportunities for teacher-candidates and their mentors (e.g., clinical teaching instructor/supervisor, clinical mentor-teachers) to engage in planning and discussion of instructional practices, to develop a deeper understanding of the educational community and students, and to engage in critical reflection on how the experience of mentoring can affect one's own teaching and mentoring practices. Hence, the goal of our residency model is to create a clinically rich experience (Flessner & Lecklider, 2017), where exploratory learning and constructivist spaces are provided to cultivate a collaborative, student-centered classroom environment. This innovative model promotes inquiry-based learning and prepares twenty-first-century educators by implementing pedagogical practices that are culturally responsive.

Our shift from a traditional EPP to the residency model also brings challenges. These challenges include how to effectively define and communicate revised mentoring roles and expectations, as well as how to select mentor-teachers who are willing to engage in the cognitive and metacognitive practices necessary to be agents of change in the teaching, learning, and mentoring processes. The shift to a yearlong clinical teaching model responds to the alarming national trends of teacher attrition and retention along with the growth of ethnically, linguistically, and racially diverse student populations.

Teacher attrition and retention rates have become a crisis, as nearly 20 percent to 40 percent of new teachers leave the field within the first five years of teaching (Gray & Taie, 2015; Brown & Schainker, 2008). At the same time, classrooms are becoming more racially and ethnically diverse, with more than 76.4 million students enrolled in U.S. schools (U.S. Census Bureau, 2018), and nearly every U.S. rural, urban, and suburban community steadily becoming racially and ethnically diverse (Hawkins, 2019). Since 2014, diverse students are the new majority in the classroom, with just over 50.3 percent of students identifying as Black, Latino/a, Asian, Native Hawaiian, other Pacific Islander, American Indian/Alaska Native, or other non-White group (National Center for Educational Statistics, 2015).

Thus, to address these issues and to ensure educational equity, selecting qualified mentor-teachers and building effective mentoring relationships is required. This process, however, takes time and starts with mutual understanding of goals, roles, responsibilities, and expectations. In traditional EPPs, the clinical teaching experience has been one semester long, requirements for qualified mentor-teachers are provided by the state board of education, and districts have their own processes for selecting qualified teachers to serve as mentor-teachers.

Often, the matching of a mentor-teacher with a teacher-candidate is conducted by district representatives with limited to no knowledge of the teacher-candidate, aside from their intended area of certification. Unless the mentor-teacher and the teacher-candidate worked together during a field experience in previous semesters, they most likely will be introduced when the teacher-candidate first reports to their assigned campus. During the traditional clinical experience, the roles, expectations, and guidelines are provided by the EPP in the form of a handbook, an online training module, and an orientation led by the clinical teaching supervisor and director of clinical teaching.

Though this traditional model fulfills requirements, research shows that it could be improved to enhance the experience for both the teacher-candidate and their mentor-teacher (Flessner & Lecklider, 2017; Klein, Taylor, Onore, Strom, & Abrams, 2013). In contrast, in the residency program, teacher-candidates spend purposefully extended time on a campus engaged in a variety of co-teaching structures with their mentor-teachers. Additionally, district partners and EPP representatives collaborate to carefully select and screen mentor-teachers, based on the mentor-teachers' knowledge of mentoring and coaching of effective pedagogical exemplars.

It is critical to set shared expectations of roles and responsibilities, provide multiple platforms for reflection on teaching practices, and match teacher-candidates and mentor-teachers based on cultural, linguistic, and ethno-racial identifiers, as well as similar interests, teaching philosophy, and certification areas (Flores et al., 2018). Thus, a purposeful teacher placement should provide a learning environment to augment the experiences of the mentor-teacher and the teacher-candidate, thereby promoting in-depth relationships that support growth for both the expert and the novice (Burns & Badiali, 2018).

Theoretical Framework

Our theoretical framework for mentoring to support the development of teachers is grounded on the Culturally Efficacious Evolution Model (CEEM) (Flores, Claeys, & Gist, 2018), which is situated within a socioconstructivist-transformative lens drawing from Vygotskian (1978) and Freirean theories (1993). Similar to Wang and Odell's (2007) suggestions, we believe that to support teachers' developmental needs, mentoring and coaching must be integrative of humanistic, situated apprenticeship, and critical constructivist approaches. Also, the holistic stance of the CEEM should be used, in which knowledge is shared, socially constructed, and mediated within the social context (Lave & Wenger, 1991), thereby promoting a continuous transformation within a community of practice in which anti-dialogical thinking and critical consciousness is valued (Freire, 1993).

The following salient proficiencies drawn from Flores et al.'s (2018) notion of cultural efficaciousness, nurtured our own development in mentoring the teacher-mentors:

1. Is self-reflective on personal (cultural, ethnic/racial, gender, spiritual) and professional (teacher, leader) identities and how these impact beliefs, positionality, and role;
2. Models critical thinking and problem-solving skills;
3. Advocates for the cultural and linguistic values of students, teachers, and their communities;
4. Facilitates the understanding of the interaction occurring among cognition, culture, and language within the sociocultural learning context and supports resiliency among diverse groups;
5. Implements mentoring and coaching techniques that embrace the concepts of cultural and critical transformative pedagogy;
6. Supports educators exploring their personal and professional identities; and
7. Guides educators through their zones of professional development to assist their quest to become culturally efficacious teachers.

Drawing on this model and the interplay of the multifaceted implementation of the TRM 2.0, Assistant Professors in Practice (APiPs) engaged in an iterative process that included reflection on their own personal and professional roles required while mentoring the mentors. In the subsequent section, we outline the program.

Program Background and Components

Integrating our theoretical framework as well as the teacher residency research (Flessner, & Lecklider, 2017) along with the needs of our teacher-candidates, the program at large, and the schools and students in our community, the TRM 2.0 was created to expand on the traditional teacher preparation program. The ultimate outcome is to graduate teachers who are able to meet the educational needs of culturally and linguistically diverse communities from day one.

The TRM 2.0 includes university and district representatives who collaborate regularly to identify employment shortage areas and discuss projected needs based on global, regional, and local factors. Through these collaborative efforts, the university and its district partners have created individualized programs that follow the model's framework. Each program within the model is specifically tailored to maximize district and university resources and address campus needs while maintaining a culturally efficacious lens. A key component to implementing the model's framework in each program is the inclusion of the role of clinical faculty—in our case, an APiP.

Specifically, APiPs facilitate mentorship by fostering a space for broader perspectives to emerge to support continued professional learning for the mentor-teacher, and to guide the novice to be successful as a new classroom teacher-leader (Achinstein & Anthanases, 2005; Childre & Van Rie, 2015; Hudson, 2007). APiPs build trust, or *confianza* (Zentella, 2005), that positively contributes to the learning and growth of mentor-teachers, teacher-candidates, students, and the APiPs themselves. In the yearlong residency program within the TRM 2.0, APiPs are embedded in the residency campus with the teacher-candidate.

APiPs offer university courses, model culturally efficacious practices, conduct research, and provide on-site support to mentor-teachers, teacher-candidates, and campus administrators. With extended time on campus through the yearlong experience, all parties are positioned to maximize professional growth, and teacher-candidates are immersed in a clinically rich and embedded model. APiPs are able to expand opportunities to interact with the mentor-teachers, teacher-candidates are able to apply what they are learning in real time and context, mentor-teachers are provided with continuous on-site support, and the APiPs are able to use the campus as a resource of examples to guide and enrich classroom discussions.

From the teacher-candidate's perspective, the TRM 2.0 provides them with time to observe, practice, and reflect on culturally efficacious classroom practices. The teacher-candidates are also able to collaborate with peers and mentor-teachers through working within a cohort at the same site. TRM 2.0 teacher-candidates shadow, co-teach, and co-plan while under the constant and consistent guidance of APiPs, mentor-teachers, and campus administrators.

From the perspective of the mentor-teachers, the yearlong residency experience has multiple benefits. Primarily, the residency program provides mentor-teachers with more opportunities to model effective practices and develop coaching relationships with their teacher-candidates, which helps improve instruction to classroom students. Secondarily, with the addition of the APiPs' presence on campus, the mentor-teachers have a fellow educator who is fully invested in the professional learning of their teacher-candidate. The APiP is available to share ideas, celebrate accomplishments, and communicate concerns in a timely manner. In addition, the presence of a residency cohort allows for engagement within a community of practice; therefore, teacher-candidates and mentor-teachers can critically reflect on their experiences.

Noteworthy, Brinson and Kottler (1993) argue that the mentor-teacher needs to develop a working knowledge of the teacher-candidate's culture and worldview. This understanding is deepened when the mentor-teacher is aware of the various "funds of knowledge" (Moll, Amanti, Neff, & Gonzalez, 1992) to which the teacher-candidate can access. Therefore, the task of the APiP within a residency program is to attain both personal and professional knowledge about the candidates through observation and interaction. This knowledge then informs the APiP of the type of coaching, mentoring, and support that will further elevate the capacity of the teacher-candidate to be culturally efficacious.

Outcomes and Learning

Three major outcomes and learning that emerged from the APiPs' critical reflections on their own mentoring development, opportunities, and practices include (1) the need for clearly defined goals, roles, and expectations; (2) the importance of developing trusting relationships; and (3) time reserved for ongoing critical reflection, collaboration, analysis, and advocacy. Included below are segments from APiPs' critical reflections on the process of becoming mentors and mentoring others.

Goals, roles, and expectations. The expressed university goal was to develop and implement an innovative residency model. APiPs were provided research readings as well professional learning opportunities for redesigning education preparation programs. While this provided some foundational knowledge, a shared goal for mentoring the mentor-teachers was not defined beyond state guidelines. Clear expectations were not delineated initially, as the TRM 2.0 was in its infancy and many of its facets were being implemented simultaneously utilizing an iterative approach designing, developing, executing, assessing, and refining it. APiPs' critical reflections revealed that they carefully negotiated their roles as mentors as Megan, an APiP, ruminates:

Without clearly stated expectations, the first year of the residency program was a series of asking for guidance, trying things out, looking for reassurance of alignment, asking for forgiveness, and celebrating successes. Though challenging, this experience contributed to my professional growth by forcing me to apply my previous experiences, analyze how they aligned with the current situation, create materials to define and communicate the vision and purpose as I understood it, listen to the needs of the people I was working with, and create structures of support that were meaningful and relevant to their experiences, to facilitate their growth and success.

A benefit of this open approach to defining goals when implementing the TRM 2.0 was the space for innovation. In regard to creating and communicating goals with mentor-teachers and campus administrators, APiPs were challenged by their positionality.

APiPs did not want to come across as imposing outside goals and agendas while attempting to teach already seasoned, highly qualified mentor-teachers. The residency model was intended to be a collaborative process with equal input from mentor-teachers and APiPs as teacher educators. Thus, all participants were required to reframe their own identities as educators. As Linda, an APiP, reflects,

> It was a challenge at times to truly comprehend what our role at the schools was not just with the mentor-teacher, but with other teachers, staff, and administrators. There was no ice breaker, and as soon as the academic year began, we were already immersed in the different schools with our teacher-candidates attempting to build relationships with all parties at the schools. These constructs sometimes allotted for high-stress situations where we felt out-of-place, but it also allowed us to frame our experiences using a culturally efficacious lens where building social interactions were essential not only for our peace of mind, but also for cultivating our professional role as an APiP and our personal role as an ally to the teacher-candidate, mentor-teacher, and school.

Through the co-construction of the goals and roles, a trusting relationship had the opportunity to form and allowed for achieving programmatic goals.

Developing trusting relationships. Development of trusting relationships was an essential and important step in the APiPs' mentoring role. As Megan noted in her critical reflection:

> The act of being available and responsive for all the little things built the trust that was vital to the teacher-candidates knowing that I heard them, saw them, understood what they were going through, and believed in them and their capacity as professionals. They also knew by my responses and actions that I would advocate for them while also teaching them how to advocate for themselves.

Eliza, another APiP, summarized the importance of a trusting reciprocal relationship through her reflective comment:

> A trusting reciprocal relationship is imperative in helping the mentor-teachers to not only feel a sense of comfort, but providing them with the time and safe space to vent and decompress the challenges they face as teachers and mentors themselves.

Hence, the flexibility in the APiP's role within the model provided necessary time and space to build trusting relationships.

Purposeful time spent on reflection, collaboration, and analysis. As APiPs, we formed a community of practice to reflect on our roles and identity. Our identity development as mentors occurred through meeting, talking, and sharing experiences within the community of practice. This space allowed the APiPs to unpack the importance of their work and to provide feedback in an environment in which all participants reflected on their own identities, advancing together in shared and articulated goals to support mentor-teachers and their teacher-candidates. For example, Megan contemplated:

> By engaging with this expanded community of practice through carefully crafted discussions and reflective experiences, I have increased my understanding of what culturally efficacious practices are, and how my identity as a culturally efficacious educator is being further developed. Through my various roles as an APiP (instructor, mentor to mentor-teachers, mentor to teacher-candidates, member of APiP group, participant in PLCs, non-tenure track faculty member), I am engaging in the process of being mentored, mentoring others, and also mentoring myself, thus enacting my socially constructed culturally efficacious identity.

Linda further stated:

> The PLCs provided opportunities for me to build better rapport with the teacher-candidates and tap into their socio-emotional assets by not only discussing shared readings, but also talking about current events, family, pressures, and other topics relevant to them. . . . By having our regular book study PLC, I was able to practice a type of humanizing pedagogy (Bartolome, 1994) where teacher-candidates were able to reflect on their own social, cultural, and linguistic resources and see how they were using them in the classrooms to establish better connections with their students. The teacher-candidates were able to translate the case studies of the four culturally efficacious teachers we read about in the book to real-world application and made connections between the theory and its integration to their immediate classrooms.

In building relationships, Eliza emphasized the importance of listening: "Honoring the mentor-teachers meant listening to their various ideas, teaching practices, and learning from their diverse backgrounds in the course of conducting observations and holding debriefing sessions in and out of professional learning communities."

Carolina's reflection also touches on the need for sensitivity to approaching discussions on various teaching practices and perspectives when building rapport between APiPs and mentor-teachers:

> Mentor-teachers, as employees of their district, must follow certain curricular programs and models. As a visitor on their campus, I have found that there has to be a balance between how I approach any questions I may have about their practice and/or questioning their ways of teaching. As part of our college's vision, we want to develop future teachers who will be "Agents of Change." It is my responsibility to also provide this learning opportunity to the mentor-teacher to assure that they can model this for our teacher-candidates so that they can apply this as they work with the students in their classroom.

Building trust and rapport naturally led to more effective collaborative efforts among APiPs, mentor-teachers, and teacher-candidates. Part of the collaborative efforts as APiPs with mentor-teachers occurred in indirect ways through mutual work with teacher-candidates. Critical consciousness and empowerment occurred in mutually beneficial ways (Freire, 1993).

As both time and responsive availability became a norm of the TRM 2.0, the teacher-candidates felt that they were acknowledged, heard, and understood. This cyclical and transformative mentoring process required knowledge acquisition of all stakeholders to invest in learning skills and tools to provide support, structure, and resiliency for the teacher-candidates. To further the growth of the mentor-teachers, time and ongoing communications in real time with teacher-candidates was required.

Purposefully created communities of practice foster culturally safe spaces for mentoring. Nurturing the mentoring relationships requires a careful crafting and balancing of multiple roles at the same time. As Linda reflected, "It is imperative that the mentor-teacher[s] and I work together as 'learning and teaching' partners and work toward supporting our teacher-candidate."

The APiPs spent time learning ways to provide opportunities, examples, and clear communication to grow as culturally efficacious practitioners invested in providing teaching and support to diverse learners. As a critical component, the community of practice experiences and reflective practices allowed for the APiPs to become culturally efficacious with the capacity and confidence to guide diverse mentor-teachers and teacher-candidates in acquiring critical and culturally transformative practices.

IMPLICATIONS FOR SUPPORTING CULTURALLY EFFICACIOUS TEACHERS AND MENTORSHIP DEVELOPMENT

If our purpose is to be agents of change, it is imperative that the change is transformational, flexible, relevant, and sustainable. The TRM 2.0 is an example of how a clinically rich, context-embedded, collaborative, and purposefully reflective culturally efficacious educator preparation program can provide space to design, develop, and expand mentoring capacity. Our TRM 2.0 is generative and organic in development, allowing for intentional and innovative expansion.

Based on our experiences implementing the program, three major recommendations for school district administrators and university leadership are made: (1) clearly define expectations for all aspects of the model; (2) be transparent with stakeholders about how roles fit into visions for the campus, the community, the district, and the university; and (3) provide space and time for critical reflection through purposefully constructed communities of practice and professional learning communities.

Goals should be specific while allowing room for interpretation, innovation, and growth within specific contexts. Just as teachers scaffold instruction for students, educators need to be provided structures that support their development as mentor-teachers. Flexibility in implementation will enable campuses and districts to meet their needs; nevertheless, overarching goals should provide foundational structures to replicate the model and commence the work.

There is also a need for transparency; each partner within the community of practice has goals and objectives to meet their respective missions. For the collaborative partnership to be successful, all parties need to have a shared understanding of how their unique goals and objectives align collectively and with those of the model overall. In this way, reciprocal partnerships can more effectively achieve their mutual goals.

It is imperative that educators are provided with space and time for relevant and meaningful critical reflection through purposefully constructed communities of practice and professional learning communities. There is a high need for district and campus administrators to provide greater cultural efficacious learning opportunities to mentor-teachers and campus teachers. The administrators must also help teachers meet and acquire the transformative practices required to meet the needs of culturally and linguistically diverse learners and to keep pace with global changes in demographic shifts in the twenty-first century.

REFERENCES

Achinstein, B., & Athanases, S. Z. (2005). Focusing new teachers on diversity and equity: Towards a knowledge base for mentors. *Teacher and Teacher Education, 21*, 843–62.

Bartolome, L. (1994). Beyond the methods fetish: Toward a humanizing pedagogy. *Harvard Educational Review, 64*(2), 173–95.

Brown, K. M., & Schainker, S. A. (2008). Doing all the right things: Teacher retention issues. *Journal of Cases in Educational Leadership, 11*(1), 10–17. https://doi.org/10.1177/1555458908325045.

Brinson, J. A., & Kottler, J. A. (1993). Cross-cultural mentoring in counselor education: a strategy for retaining minority faculty. *Counselor Education & Supervision, 32*(4), 241–53. doi:10.1002/j.1556-6978.1993.tb00252.x.

Burns, R. W., & Badiali, B. J. (2018). Clinical pedagogy and pathways of clinical pedagogical practice: A conceptual framework for teaching about teaching in clinical experiences. *Action in Teacher Education 40*(4) 428–46. doi:10.1080/01626620.2018.1503978.

Childre, A. L., & Van Rie, G. L. (2015). Mentor teacher training: A hybrid model to promote partnering in candidate development. *Rural Special Education Quarterly 34*(1), 10–16.

Flessner, R. & Lecklider, D. R. (Eds.) (2017). *The power of clinical preparation in teacher education.* Lanham, MD: Rowman & Littlefield.

Flores, B., Gist, C., & Claeys, L. (2018). *Crafting culturally efficacious teacher preparation and pedagogies.* Lanham, MD: Rowman & Littlefield.

Freire, P. (1993). *Pedagogy of the oppressed.* New York, NY: Continuum.

Gardiner, W. (2011). Mentoring in an urban teacher residency: Mentors' perceptions of yearlong placements. *The New Educator, 7*(2), 153–71.

Gray, L., & Taie, S. (2015). *Public school teacher attrition and mobility in the first five years: Results from the first through fifth waves of the 2007–08 Beginning Teacher Longitudinal Study (NCES 2015-337).* Washington, DC: U.S. Department of Education, National Center for Education Statistics. Retrieved from http://nces.ed.gov/pubs2015/2015337.pdf.

Hawkins, B. D. (2019). *Diverse student populations are in the classroom: Are you prepared to meet their needs?* Washington, DC: National Educational Association. Retrieved from http://www.nea.org/home/66241.htm.

Hudson, P. (2007). Examining mentors' practices for enhancing preservice teachers' pedagogical development in mathematics and science. *Mentoring & Tutoring, 15*(2), 201–17.

Klein, E.J., Taylor, M., Onore, C., Strom, K., & Abrams, L. (2013) Finding a third space in teacher education: creating an urban teacher residency, *Teaching Education, 24*(1), 27–57, doi:10.1080/10476210.2012.711305.

Lave, J., & Wenger, E. (1991). *Situated learning legitimate peripheral participation.* Cambridge, UK: Cambridge University Press.

Moll, L. C., Amanti, C., Neff, D., & Gonzalez, N. (1992). Funds of knowledge for teaching: Using a qualitative approach to connect homes and classrooms. *Theory Into Practice, 31*(2), 132–141. doi:10.1080/00405849209543534.

National Center for Educational Statistics (2015). https://nces.ed.gov/programs/raceindicators/indicator_rbb.asp.

Reinhardt, K. S. (2017). Mentoring in clinical placements: Conceptualization of role and its impact on practices. *Action in Teacher Education, 39*(4), 381–96.

U. S. Census Bureau. (2018). *More than 76 million students enrolled in U.S. schools, Census Bureau reports.* Retrieved from https://www.census.gov/newsroom/press-releases/2018/school-enrollment.html.

Vygotsky, L. S. (1978). *Mind in society: The development of higher psychological processes.* Cambridge, MA: Harvard University Press.

Wang, J., & Odell, S. J. (2007). An alternative conception of mentor–novice relationships: Learning to teach in reform-minded ways as a context. *Teaching and Teacher Education, 23*(4), 473–89. doi:10.1016/j.tate.2006.12.010.

Zentella, A. (2005). Building on strengths *con educacion, respecto, y confianza* [with education, respect, and trust]. In A. Zentella (Ed.) *Building on strength: Language and literacy in Latino families and communities*, (pp. 175–82). New York, NY: Teachers College Press.

Chapter Seven

The Identification, Selection, and Evaluation of Mentor-Teachers within a Professional Development School Setting

Timothy Lintner, PhD; Bridget Coleman, PhD; Jeremy Rinder, MS; Deborah McMurtrie, PhD; University of South Carolina Aiken

There presently exists a concerted body of research that explores the conceptual and theoretical underpinnings of Professional Development Schools (PDS) (Garin, et al., 2015; Kolpin, Shoemaker, & Cosenza, 2015; Polly, Smaldino, & Brynteson, 2015) as well as individual configurations of PDS models in action (Bebas, 2016; Pepper, Hartman, & Blackwell, 2012; Young, Cavanaugh, & Moloney, 2018). From available classroom space to various forms of collaboration, a subset of this literature highlights the focused strategies that make PDS partnerships both responsive and effective (Ikpeze, Broikou, & Hildenbrand, 2012; Jones, Schwerdtfeger, Roop, & Long, 2016; Mark, 2017). Yet missing from the literature is, arguably, one of the most important pieces to any successful school-university PDS partnership: the identification, selection, and evaluation of mentor-teachers. Simply, what is the criteria used to identify school-based mentor-teachers to assist in the preparation of teacher-candidates?

This chapter will examine best practice in mentor-teacher identification, selection, and evaluation. Findings will be contextualized within a case study focusing on the decade-old PDS partnership between J. D. Lever Elementary School and the School of Education at the University of South Carolina Aiken. An examination of the evolution, if you will, of mentor-teacher identification, selection, and evaluation will be discussed, paying particular attention to the changing needs of the university and the changing personnel dynamics at J. D. Lever Elementary School. Subsequent recommendations will be made that provide guidance in facilitating and sustaining a productive, collaborate, and dynamic PDS partnership.

MENTORING WITHIN A PROFESSIONAL DEVELOPMENT SCHOOL SETTING

Professional Development Schools (PDS) are positively affecting how teacher-candidates are trained (Aldrich, 2001; Cobb, 2000; NCATE, 2010). The very nature of the PDS model is transforming the ways in which schools and school districts and colleges of education partner to provide innovative, hands-on teaching and learning experiences in K–12 classrooms (Polizzi, 2009). Such partnerships directly impact teacher-candidate confidence and competence and, in turn, directly affect student learning (Wasieleweski & Gahlsdorf Terrell, 2014).

Integral to the successful design and implementation of any PDS model is the role of the mentor-teacher. Inherent here is what defines constructive and effective mentoring. Zembytska (2015) posits that teacher-candidate mentoring should constitute a mutually beneficial, formal collaboration between the mentor-teacher and the teacher-candidate, whereby the mentor-teacher gains new pedagogical ideas and strategies and the teacher-candidate gains invaluable insight and hands-on instructional practice.

Specifically, mentor-teachers should be able to articulate (explain) and demonstrate (model) the principles of effective teaching and learning both inside and outside of the classroom (Sheridan & Young, 2017; Timperley, 2001). Mentor-teachers should provide teacher-candidates with timely, constructive, and honest feedback in a caring and empathetic manner. Not only does effective mentoring introduce and expose teacher-candidates to the "real world" of teaching, but it also increases motivation while concomitantly facilitating generally positive attitudes toward teaching and the teaching profession. With a working definition of effective mentoring in hand, two pressing questions remain: What demonstrable qualities should a mentor-teacher possess? And after identification, how are mentor-teachers subsequently selected to participate and ultimately evaluated?

The establishment and sustainability of our USC Aiken Professional Development Schools (PDS) has proven to be one of our most distinguished endeavors. We started the innovative initiative over a decade ago, desiring to move our educational methods courses from campus classrooms to local public schools. Premised on the need to enhance teacher-candidate preparation with more robust, diverse, and sustained field-based experiences, the USC Aiken School of Education developed a fledgling partnership with a single local school, J. D. Lever Elementary School.

THE IDENTIFICATION AND SELECTION OF MENTOR-TEACHERS

The identification and selection of a quality mentor-teacher is the most critical component in ensuring a successful clinical experience for our teacher-candidates within a Professional Development School setting. This importance is reflected in the Council for the Accreditation of Educator Preparation (CAEP) indicator 2.2, which emphasizes the importance of quality mentor-teachers:

> Partners co-select, prepare, evaluate, support, and retain high-quality clinical educators, both provider- and school-based, who demonstrate a positive impact on candidates' development and P–12 student learning and development. In collaboration with their partners, providers use multiple indicators and appropriate technology-based applications to establish, maintain, and refine criteria for selection, professional development, performance evaluation, continuous improvement, and retention of clinical educators in all clinical placement settings. (http://caepnet.org)

Since the inception of our PDS partnership with J. D. Lever Elementary School, we have sought two levels or tiers of assistance from our mentor-teachers. Mentor-teachers working with freshman- and sophomore-level teacher-candidates are asked to provide structured access to their classroom. Mentoring is informal, consisting mainly of providing insight and context when warranted.

Mentor-teachers working with junior- and senior-level teacher-candidates assume a larger, more structured, and concerted role; they are expected to actively mentor and coach their assigned teacher candidate, provide guidance and support in lesson planning, facilitate direct instruction opportunities, provide substantive verbal and written feedback on a regular basis, and allow university-based teacher educators access to their classrooms to evaluate the assigned teacher-candidate's instructional ability.

During the first year or two, we identified and selected mentor-teachers, not premised on the CAEP standards outlined above; we sought assistance from teachers we personally knew who possessed high-quality reputations and positive working relationships with students, teachers, and administrators. There was no established process in identifying possible mentor-teachers. This casual, collegial, yet somewhat unstructured process initially "worked" as virtually everyone we approached was excited about the innovative PDS model and agreed to serve as a mentor-teacher. We soon came to realize that although we knew our mentor-teachers personally, we had limited knowledge of their teaching styles and mentoring skills.

To provide a much-needed measure of assurance in identifying and selecting possible mentor-teachers, we implemented two structures of support: one processional, the other philosophical. Before we personally reached out to potential mentor-teachers, we contacted the building principal to provide a list of whom he/she thought would be exemplar (and willing) mentor-teachers. This gave us another reference point in identifying possible mentor-teachers.

We also worked to identify desirable personal and professional characteristics that defined an effective mentor and, (hopefully) concomitantly, effective mentoring. We invested significant time building and maintaining positive, collegial relationships with our partnering teachers, knowing that there were varying levels of mentoring experience. With the principal's suggested list of potential mentor-teachers in hand, we sought to identify and ultimately select mentor-teachers who possessed and demonstrated the following traits: strong interpersonal and communication skills; exceptional organizational and time management acumen; sound pedagogical and content knowledge; ability to inspire, support, and motivate others; and, lastly, an unwavering commitment to excellence in teaching.

Premised on instructional observations by university faculty coupled with the feedback provided by the first few cohorts of teacher-candidates, it became clear early on that many, but not all, in our mentor-teacher pool exhibited the pedagogical and structural tools needed to support teacher-candidate success. A few struggled with effective mentoring. Over time, some mentor-teachers who initially struggled were able to gain the requisite skills and dispositions to indeed become effective mentors.

Others realized this was not their area of strength and opted not to continue in this role. Though personally uncomfortable, we have periodically had to "release" a handful of mentor-teachers. In doing so, we put our personal relationships aside while remaining steadfast in our commitment to placing our teacher-candidates with the most caring and capable mentor-teachers. In our quest to do so, we often returned to the same mentor-teachers each semester.

Through the years, we have admittedly had to compromise when making select teacher-candidate placements. Ideally, we strive to make one-to-one placements: one mentor-teacher working with one teacher-candidate. When the number of teacher-candidates in each semester exceeded the number of identified and selected mentor-teachers, we have reached out to teachers who are accessible but not outstanding.

In such situations, we often placed our most capable teacher-candidates (e.g., mature, confident, possessing excellent written and communication skills, capable of producing sound lesson design and delivery) with such "accessible" mentor-teachers. In some cases, however, we simply would not compromise, and we placed two teacher-candidates with a single mentor-teacher. Both scenarios are admittedly not ideal. Yet we continually weigh the needs of the university with the dynamics of our PDS partner. Though we have strategically (and successfully) worked to refine the process in which we identify and ultimately select caring and capable mentor-teachers, what was glaringly missing from our PDS partnership was a quantifiable way in which to evaluate them.

THE EVALUATION OF MENTOR-TEACHERS

As we continue to refine our Professional Development School relationship with J. D. Lever Elementary School and expand our PDS initiatives to other area partner schools, one of our primary goals is the development and implementation of a systematic evaluation of selected mentor-teachers. By having a concrete evaluative process in place, we can provide our teacher-candidates with in-class experiences that are positive, constructive, and supportive. To this end, we are working to facilitate effective partnerships between teacher-candidates and mentor-teachers by establishing criteria for vetting teachers, utilizing evaluation data, and working to match philosophies of education.

TEACHER-CANDIDATE EVALUATION OF MENTOR-TEACHERS

We have taken a major step forward by incorporating a process by which teacher-candidates evaluate their mentor-teachers. Though we implemented a similar practice early in our PDS partnership, the "evaluation" generally consisted of a series of open-ended, non-confidential questions asked at the end of the term: "Did you like working with your mentor-teacher?" "Should we use him/her next semester?" Though useful at the time, such questions netted us little information other than subjective, often knee-jerk responses. We realized that we needed more detailed insight from our teacher-candidates in order to make informed decisions regarding whom to select as a mentor-teacher.

The process by which teacher-candidates evaluate their mentor-teachers was born out of a similar tool that was used for teacher-candidates during their internship experience. At the end of their internship semester, teacher-candidates were given a survey that asked them to evaluate and, ultimately, recommend (or not) their respective mentor-teacher. The survey results provided invaluable—and honest—data about our selected mentor-teachers.

We took this same concept and created an online survey that teacher-candidates in our Professional Development School now complete at the end of all practicum courses prior to their internship experience. This evaluative survey allows teacher-candidates to rate their mentor-teachers in key areas such as learning environment, instructional practices, management, feedback, and diversity. Finally, each teacher-candidate can recommend (or not) the use of their mentor-teacher in the future.

All questions are supported by open-ended responses. Survey data reveals that roughly 94 percent of teacher-candidates would recommend the continued use of their mentor-teacher. Teacher-candidates generally felt that mentor-teachers positively modeled effective classroom management strategies as well as worked to develop a positive, helpful relationship with them. Conversely, teacher-candidates indicated that mentor-teachers struggled to create and implement strategies to effectively engage all students in their respective classrooms.

UNIVERSITY EVALUATION OF MENTOR-TEACHERS

In order to have a comprehensive evaluation of mentor-teachers, it is also critical that the university-based teacher educators have the opportunity to provide structured input. In the past, university-based teacher educators have simply made recommendations about the use of mentor-teachers either through email and/or casual, often spontaneous departmental debriefings. The goal, however, was to move beyond this informal and often cursory evaluation and implement a systematic method for allowing an evidence-based evaluation of the mentor-teacher(s) they partner with on behalf of our teacher-candidates. Mirroring the mentor-teacher survey teacher-candidates now complete, this online survey is completed at the conclusion of each semester and asks university-based teacher educators to rate mentor-teachers using the same key areas found in the student survey.

In conjunction with the survey, university-based teacher educators across our PDS sites use a rubric to evaluate practicum and internship-based mentor-teachers. The rubric evaluates select qualities and practices (recommended, willing, experienced, trained, positive, inclusive, structured, organized, knowledgeable, skilled) scored on a 10-point Likert scale. Anecdotal evidence is provided to support their ratings, and an overall recommendation is provided as well.

We have spent roughly a decade building a strong and collaborative relationship with our J. D. Lever Elementary School PDS partner, and we have been open and transparent regarding potential or actualized modifications made in the selection, identification, and evaluation of mentor-teachers. Yet with our mentor-teachers undergoing two evaluations—one by the teacher-candidate and now one by the university-based teacher educator—we had to be sensitive to the other layers, if you will, of evaluation our mentor-teachers underwent at the building, district, and state levels.

Though important for our teacher-candidates, we soon realized that we had inadvertently created a scenario by which our mentor-teachers might feel increasingly "under the microscope." Balancing the need for selecting strong mentor-teachers without disrupting our appreciation for their dedication to the program is a hurdle that we are beginning to work through as we continue to build capacity for evaluating mentor-teachers.

EXPANDING REQUIREMENTS

One of the benefits of the Professional Development School model is the strong relationship established between the faculty and staff of the School of Education at USC Aiken and the administration at J. D. Lever Elementary School. Housing undergraduate methods courses within the partner school ensures that this relationship is natural and allows for open professional dialogue. As implemented in the second year of our partnership, we continue to rely on building administrators for an initial screening of mentor-teachers. We never use a mentor-teacher without principal approval. Conversely, we never use a mentor-teacher "assigned" by the principal without their consent.

One of our ongoing goals is to help principals select quality mentor-teachers. We continue to seek mentor-teachers who are willing and interested in serving as well as possessing the aforementioned personal and professional characteristics of effective communication skills, organizational prowess, firm content knowledge, and advocacy both inside and outside of the classroom. We now require that all selected mentor-teachers have at least two years of teaching experience in the appropriate certification area or specified grade level.

We also established a practice that selected mentor-teachers must be trained in the present tool used to evaluate all South Carolina educators, South Carolina Teaching Standards 4.0 (SCTS 4.0). It is critical for our mentor-teachers to be experienced in using this tool, as it will be used both during teacher-candidate internship and, most importantly, during their own professional career. To both streamline and expedite the training process, certified faculty in the School of Education train mentor-teachers on how to use SCTS 4.0. The School of Education has also utilized online refresher courses and evaluation calibration modules to help ensure that our mentor-teachers are confident in evaluating their teacher-candidates.

SURVEY DATA

In addition to the requirements noted above, we intentionally use the data collected through our evaluation surveys to assist in the selection of mentor-teachers at J. D. Lever Elementary School. All teacher-candidate, mentor-teacher, and university-based teacher educator surveys are closely reviewed upon the culmination of all methods courses and at the completion of teacher-candidate internship experiences.

In the case that a mentor-teacher has been identified as not possessing the desired standards of effective mentorship, the director of field experiences contacts either the teacher-candidate or the university-based teacher educator to garner additional insight as to the decision provided. This secondary, more explicit input is used to help ensure that a mentor-teacher is not excluded based on personality conflicts or general misunderstandings of expectations or outcomes. This multi-level evaluative process ensures that continuing partnerships—or the release thereof—with selected mentor-teachers is rooted more in triangulated evidence than unimodal subjectivity.

Using the results of our accumulated survey data has allowed us to build a database of mentor-teachers to consider (or not) when making practicum or internship placements for our teacher-candidates. This database is maintained on a secure drive and available to all faculty within the School of Education. (This database includes mentor-teachers from J. D. Lever Elementary School and our other twelve PDS partners.) Such data now affords easy, reliable access to a consistent core of vetted mentor-teachers, which will, in partnership with faculty in the School of Education, ensure that our teacher-candidates are well prepared for their chosen profession.

PHILOSOPHIES OF EDUCATION

A final strategy we recently implemented was to intentionally match teacher-candidates with mentor-teachers who share their philosophy of education. Teacher-candidates are given a short one-question survey that lists four broad philosophies of education and provides a short description of each:

- *Essentialism:* teacher-centered philosophy in which the fundamental role of education is to teach fundamental concepts of academic knowledge and

character development. This philosophy is often characterized by highly structured classrooms and instructional strategies such as lecturing and note-taking.
- *Perennialism:* teacher-centered philosophy in which the fundamental role of education is to teach students timeless and traditional academic content. This philosophy is often characterized by the use of traditional instructional strategies with an emphasis on reasoning and vocational development.
- *Progressivism:* student-centered philosophy in which the fundamental role of education is to develop the whole child. This philosophy is characterized by providing students with meaningful experiences and is often associated with problem-based and project-based learning.
- *Existentialism:* student-centered philosophy in which the fundamental role of education is to help students develop their own interests. This philosophy is characterized by student choices and an emphasis of student development as opposed to curriculum and content.

Prior to internship, each teacher-candidate selects the philosophy that most closely aligns with their personal and professional beliefs about teaching and learning. Mentor-teachers are then given the same survey. Once baseline philosophies of educations are established for both groups, teacher-candidates are then matched with mentor-teachers who share their beliefs and attitudes about education. This strategy was initially implemented with teacher-candidates entering their internship experience. The goal is to provide teacher-candidates with a clinical experience that will most likely reflect their future classroom. Moreover, we hope that by matching philosophies, both the teacher-candidate and the mentor-teacher can create co-constructed opportunities to learn and grow from one another.

RECOMMENDATIONS AND CONCLUSION

To provide guidance for institutions who are in the process of building a PDS partnership, or for those institutions with established partnerships wishing to increase capacity for identifying, selecting, and evaluating mentor-teachers, we offer four succinct recommendations. Throughout our decade-long partnership with J. D. Lever Elementary School, these select insights have proven pivotal in how our partnership is structured, sustained, and enhanced.

- Invest time and effort in developing meaningful relationships with your PDS partners. These relationships must be nurtured to be sustained. Such

relationships require deliberate planning and ongoing attention. At its core, PDS partnerships are built on relationships.
- Not all teachers initially understand what serving as a mentor entails. Some need more time and experience to grow into highly effective mentor-teachers. Support, encouragement, and a degree of patience are imperative.
- Regular communication, shared decision-making, and flexibility are key. Communicate openly and often with your PDS partners. Be clear in your processes of identifying, selecting, and evaluating potential mentor-teachers. Share expectations—of them and of you. Encourage their ownership of the process by soliciting feedback and working to collaboratively facilitate necessary change. With changing schedules, rotating teacher-candidates, and unforeseen hiccups in the process, flexibility is a must. Flexibility is facilitated through communication and trust.
- Designate a university-based teacher educator to serve as a liaison between the college or university and your PDS partner. This liaison understands school policies and procedures, handles scheduling and logistics, and works to maintain positive working relationships with both school-based mentor-teachers and administrators. A single point-person reduces confusion and potential redundancy by funneling both messaging and program execution.

A cornerstone to providing teacher-candidates with rich and rewarding field-based experiences is the identification and selection of mentor-teachers. The evolution and resultant success of our PDS partnership is due in part to the many mentor-teachers who have dedicated their time and energy to the preparation of our teacher-candidates. The Professional Development School partnership between J. D. Lever Elementary School and the University of South Carolina Aiken has strategically worked to implement concrete steps to ensure that the most caring and competent mentor-teachers are identified, selected, and ultimately evaluated. We continue to work with our J. D. Lever Elementary School partners to refine in-place processes that encourage, structure, and sustain the professional growth of both our mentor-teachers and teacher-candidates alike.

REFERENCES

Aldrich, J. E. (2001). *Professional Development Schools: Listening to teachers' and teacher candidates' voices*. Paper presented at the Annual Meeting of the Association of Teacher Educators, August 8, 2000, Portland, OR.

Bebas, C. (2016). School-university partnerships: The Professional Development Schools model, self-efficacy, teacher efficacy, and its impact on beginning teachers. *School-University Partnerships, 9*(2), 18–27.

Council for the Accreditation of Educator Preparation (CAEP) (2013). Standard 2: Clinical Partnerships and Practice. Retrieved from: http://caepnet.org.

Cobb, J. (2000). The impact of a professional development school in preservice teacher preparation, inservice teachers' professionalism, and children's achievement: Perceptions of inservice teachers. *Action in Teacher Education, 22*(3), 64–76.

Garin, E., Taylor, T., Madden, M., Beiter, J., Davis, J., Farmer, D., & Nowlin, D. (2015). The Bowie State University Professional Development Schools Network partnership. *School-University Partnerships, 8*(2), 9–13.

Ikpeze, C. H., Broikou, K. A., & Hildenbrand, S. (2012). PDS collaboration as third space: An analysis of the quality of learning experiences in a PDS partnership. *Studying Teacher Education, 8*(3), 275–88.

Jones, J., Schwerdtfeger, S., Roop, T., & Long, J. L. (2016). Trailblazing partnerships: Professional Development Schools in partnership with Emporia State University. *School-University Partnerships, 9*(1), 7–10.

Kolpin, T., Shoemaker, E., & Cosenza, M. (2015). Concept of readiness: Assessing factors in the development, implementation, and sustainability of PDS partnership. *School-University Partnerships, 8*(1), 24–26.

Mark, K. (2017). Understanding mentoring practices in a professional development school partnership. *School-University Partnerships, 10*(2), 13–16.

National Council for the Accreditation of Teacher Education (NCATE). (2010). Transforming teacher education through clinical practice: A national strategy to prepare effective educators. Retrieved from http://ncate.org.

Pepper, S. K., Hartman, K. J., & Blackwell. S. E. (2012). Creating an environment of educational excellence: The University of Mississippi PDS partnership—the evolution continues. *School-University Partnerships, 5*(1), 74–88.

Polizzi, J. A. (2009). Best practices for transformational teacher education: The full-immersion professional development schools alternative. *School-University Partnerships, 3*(2), 98–111.

Polly, D., Smaldino, S., & Brynteson, K. (2015). Developing a rubric to support the evaluation of professional development school partnerships. *School-University Partnerships, 8*(1), 20–23.

Sheridan, L. & Young, M. (2017). Genuine conversations: The enabler of good mentoring of pre-service teachers. *Teachers and Teaching: Theory and Practice, 23*(6), 658–73.

Timperley, H. (2001). Mentoring conversations designed to promote student teacher learning. *Asia-Pacific Journal of Teacher Education, 29*(2), 111–23.

Wasieleweski, L. M., & Gahlsdorf Terrell, D. (2014). What's next? Beyond the basics of partnerships. *School-University Partnerships, 7*(2), 48–61.

Young, A., Cavanaugh, M., & Moloney, R. (2018). Building a whole school approach to professional experience: Collaboration and community. *Asia-Pacific Journal of Teacher Education, 46*(3), 279–91.

Zembytska, M. (2015). Supporting novice teachers through mentoring and induction in the United States. *Comparative Professional Pedagogy, 5*(1), 105–11.

Chapter Eight

Partners in Learning
Building Mentoring Partnerships through a Shared Learning Experience

Rachelle Curcio, PhD, University of South Carolina;
Alyson Adams, PhD, University of Florida

There is widespread agreement that the clinical internship is one of the most valuable and relevant components of teacher preparation. One key to the effectiveness of this experience is high-quality mentoring, often described as educative in nature (Bradbury & Koballa, 2008; Feiman-Nemser, 2012). While the literature outlines the importance of educative mentoring, the researchers continue to learn about ways to foster the development of these relationships and interactions.

In this study, based on a larger qualitative study (Curcio, 2017), the researchers examined how a shared learning experience prior to the clinical internship, involving interns and their mentor-teachers, was perceived by participants as contributing to the development of mentoring relationships and interactions during the internship. In particular, the participating mentor-intern pairs noted that their joint attendance at the shared learning experience contributed to an accelerated and strengthened relationship throughout the internship.

LITERATURE

Throughout the evolution of teacher education, clinical practice has been situated as a vital component of twenty-first-century teacher preparation (AACTE, 2018; NCATE, 2010). In particular, the clinical internship has often been identified as the single most influential aspect of a candidate's preparation (Wilson, Floden, & Ferrini-Mundy, 2001). Recognizing the importance of the clinical internship, Feiman-Nemser and Buchmann (1987) outlined a framework to enhance the educative nature of the internship experience. Central to this framework is the cultivation of a collaborative, guided environment in which mentor-intern pairs engage in educative mentoring.

The role of a mentor in teacher preparation is a multifaceted endeavor that greatly influences the quality of teacher-candidate learning (Zeichner, 2002). Ideally, every teacher-candidate would experience educative mentoring in which both the intern and mentor engage in professional growth. Educative mentoring extends beyond emotional and logistical support and provides opportunities for interactions focused on co-teaching, co-planning, collaborative reflection, coaching, and feedback. Such interactions engage stakeholders in the intellectual work of teaching and instill lifelong habits that foster student and teacher learning (Feiman-Nemser, 2012; Schwille, 2008).

Unfortunately, mentoring received during teacher-candidates' practicum experiences often lacks coherence and may be inconsistent across placements (Darling-Hammond, Hammerness, Grossman, Rust, & Shulman, 2005). Many interns do not develop educative mentoring relationships with their mentors, and dynamics become complicated and challenging (Bullough & Draper, 2004; Valencia, Martin, Place, & Grossman, 2009).

These challenges create tensions that stem from a lack of coherent content and pedagogical knowledge, inconsistent and superficial feedback, misaligned goals and expectations, and an inability to apply knowledge and pedagogy in mentor classrooms (Bradbury & Koballa, 2008; Valencia et al., 2009). With knowledge of mentor-teachers' influence over the "affective and intellectual tone" (Feiman-Nemser, 2012, p. 205) of the internship experience, AACTE's Clinical Practice Commission (2016) called for situating relationship development as a central component of clinical practice.

Recognizing the complexities of developing, maintaining, and sustaining educative mentoring relationships, scholars have emphasized a focus on better understanding the cultivation of productive mentor-intern relationships (Ambrosetti, Knight, & Dekkers, 2014; Hudson, 2016). In particular, recently developed hybrid, or third-space, learning experiences that bring mentors and teacher-candidates together as co-learners have been acknowledged as a space for mentor-intern pairs to foster educative relationships (AACTE, 2018; Turner & Blackburn, 2016; Zeichner, 2010).

As currently conceptualized in some teacher education literature (Flessner, 2014; Zeichner, 2010), third space is emerging to describe hybrid environments where learning can take place outside traditional learning institutions to reduce traditional hierarchies and power present in academic settings that privilege academic knowledge over practical knowledge. However, the authors argue that simply moving learning to new locations outside academia does not eliminate hierarchy or power structures, nor help teacher-candidates develop strategies for long-term school-based learning.

Furthermore, these conceptions of third space do not always include mentor-teachers in meaningful ways that focus on their own learning. Rather, they are often repositioned in new roles as experts—teachers-in-residence; contributors to course content (Zeichner, 2010)—which puts them back in a hierarchical structure, as opposed to learners in an educative environment alongside teacher-candidates. While these new roles for teachers are empowering and encouraging, the researchers feel this conception does not focus enough on mentor-teachers as learners in this third space.

Conversely, when regarded as boundary-spanning teacher educators, mentor-teachers may interact with teacher-candidates as co-learners throughout various facets of clinical practice. Moreover, while accountable for assuming the responsibilities of educative mentoring (AACTE, 2018), it is paramount that mentors act to foster productive mentor-intern relationships. Shared learning experiences can begin to lay the foundation for reciprocal mentor-intern relationships that lead to educative mentoring interactions; however, the development of hybrid co-learning experiences requires more than simply bringing mentor-intern pairs together. Recently, Canipe and Gunckel (2019) defined *co-learning experiences* as "an approach to preservice teacher preparation that is designed to engage preservice and mentor-teachers in constructing shared understandings while working together on teaching related activities" (p. 2). Thus, co-learning experiences must be intentionally designed to represent authentic tasks that value all participants' contributions (Curcio, 2017; Turner & Blackburn, 2016).

Recent literature has begun to more deeply analyze hybrid experiences that situate mentor-teachers and teacher-candidates as co-learners (Canipe & Gunckel, 2019; Gunckel & Wood, 2016; Turner & Blackburn, 2016; Wood & Turner, 2015). In particular, these studies have focused on mentors' and interns' perceptions of attending these experiences and their engagement during tasks. For example, Gunckel and Wood (2016) analyzed participants' discourse throughout a co-learning event to identify "sense making while learning together about teaching science" (p. 98). Our study examined a step further by understanding how the shared learning experience carried over to the internship.

THIS STUDY: PARTNERS IN LEARNING

This study sought to better understand the transfer of the relationships developed during a hybrid summer shared learning experience into the clinical internship classroom. The shared learning experience of interest, henceforth referred to as the "institute," was part of a larger multi-year grant from our State Department of Education. Our charge for the grant was to (1) deepen teacher-candidates' content knowledge in math, language arts, science, and social studies, (2) improve teacher-candidates' instructional practice to improve K–5 student learning, specifically in diverse high-poverty school contexts, and (3) enhance the culminating field experience, or clinical internship (Curcio, 2017). The institute supported all three grant goals by being focused on integrating content knowledge instruction for mentor-teachers and teacher-candidates and the co-creation of unit and lesson plans to be used during the internship experience to support student success.

The institute was designed to be held during the summer, prior to the yearlong clinical internship, for two weeks at a fairly neutral location: one year at the University partner school, and another year at a local middle school not involved in the elementary-focused grant. The authors chose neutral locations purposefully to allow both mentor-teachers and teacher-candidates to fully engage without the temptations of a familiar location.

University facilitators from the College of Education and Liberal Arts and Sciences (from each relevant content area) collaborated on the design and delivery of the institute content. While all teacher-candidates and mentors were invited to participate, the authors purposefully only selected to follow those who could attend in pairs because they wanted them to work together on the learning tasks.

Approximately thirty pairs attended each year, each assigned to high-poverty public schools in our local context. Mentor-teachers were paid a stipend for their time (commensurate with district funding for professional learning in the summer), and teacher-candidates attended as a part of a six-week summer course where their tuition was covered by the grant. The researchers also catered lunch for participants to keep them on-site with informal social time and because our institute was a full day, from 8 a.m. to 4 p.m. The authors understand that the provision of these institute benefits may have impacted who chose to attend and their motivations for doing so, and that funding of these benefits is not always possible for all universities on a regular basis without grant funding.

A pilot study of the institute hinted at the power of this experience, so the authors designed a study for the following year to include both the summer experience and the clinical internship. Specifically, the authors sought to identify mentor-intern pairs' perceptions regarding the relationship between attending the institute prior to the clinical internship and their mentoring interactions during the first semester of a yearlong internship.

This qualitative study consisted of four mentor-intern pairs. Through interviews, observations, and analysis of artifacts, the authors established that participants recognized several features of the summer institute as important to their mentoring relationship. First, the institute was held at a neutral context, where neither the intern nor the mentor held a position of comfort or authority. Second, the two-week duration of the institute created time and space for the pairs to work on interdisciplinary teaching tasks and get to know each other on a personal basis. And third, the institute was designed around authentic experiences that were to be used back in the classroom.

Beyond the structure of the institute, they followed the interns into the classroom to understand more about their mentoring interactions and relationships. The mentors and interns, independently, reported that the summer institute made it possible for them to hit the ground running, and to immediately value each other's expertise and trust each other to focus on student learning from day one. The mentors, having experienced other interns in the past without benefit of the summer institute, noted how the institute both accelerated and strengthened their relationships with the interns.

Institute Description

As mentioned above, there were key facets of the institute that contributed to the mentor-intern pairs' cultivation of a productive mentoring relationship. The information below describes institute components that both mentors and interns consistently referenced as influential on their clinical internship experience.

Institute Design

The institute was a mix of new learning, reflection, and creation of authentic tasks. Each day began with a reflection on the previous day's content and a connection to the new concepts. New learning was largely small bursts of classroom lectures, with demonstrations and experiments (math, science, and technology integration), guest speakers, and authentic texts (social studies and English language arts).

Approximately one-third of the time each day was spent on interactions between the pairs so that mentor-teachers and teacher-candidates could process their learning and construct activities to bring back to the classroom. The researchers used a variety of engagement strategies (e.g., jigsaw, turn and talk, gallery walks) and discussion protocols (e.g., National School Reform Faculty, 2019; School Reform Initiative, 2019) to model the same level of learner engagement they wanted to see in the final unit designs.

A very important task that extended across the entire institute was the creation of an interdisciplinary unit plan. There were daily opportunities for unit planning where mentor-intern pairs worked together and drew on the interdisciplinary content from the institute. Elements of the unit plan included selecting a grade-level appropriate standard, writing three lesson plans for the unit, the creation of a digital book using Web 2.0 tools, curating a list of resources and trade books to use during the unit, drafting a parent communication about the unit and how to extend learning into the home, and the creation of a publicly shared website that highlighted the pairs' overall understanding of interdisciplinary teaching. Lastly, all mentor-intern pairs collaboratively presented their units showcase-style on the final day of the institute.

Depth of Content

The authors faced two challenges related to institute content. Because they wanted this to be a shared learning experience where mentor-intern pairs were co-learners, they had to present learning that was more complex and advanced. They also had the challenge of needing to support teachers from the range of elementary grades, K–5. In year one, they separated K–2 and 3–5 teachers and teacher-candidates with slightly modified content (math/science/technology) via rotating stations throughout the entirety of the institute.

However, in year two, they brought all participants together around advanced social studies content in the morning, and then differentiated English Language Arts content in the afternoon by K–2 and 3–5. Technology was integrated throughout both content areas.

Regarding social studies, they focused on controversial issues related to the essential question of "What is a citizen?" and covered local school segregation issues from the sixties to current controversies with immigrants and DACA.

In English Language Arts, they employed Writer's Workshop, where participants had to engage in all aspects of the writing process around the essential question of "How has citizenship been a part of your life story?" These more advanced topics allowed both sets of participants to bring something to the table, conceptually, and yet also be learners themselves in many ways. An unintended consequence of the focus on citizenship allowed personal matters to surface, leading to our next section on building relationships during the institute.

BUILDING RELATIONSHIPS BEYOND CONTENT LEARNING

In year one, with the focus on advanced learning in math and science, the authors found that participants bonded over helping each other learn more complicated topics that some had not yet tackled. For example, several mentor-teachers were not familiar with the 5E model (Engage, Explore, Explain, Elaborate, Evaluate) of science instruction or the incorporation of accountable talk in mathematics, both topics that teacher-candidates had been previously exposed to within methods coursework.

But in year two, with the focus on citizenship, many pairs opened up to each other through poetry and prose about challenging personal issues that helped them understand each other as human beings, or that created tensions that we had to facilitate and manage toward resolution. The content of year two was much more personal and emotional, as participants spent time writing, peer editing and revising, and then discussing how to bring elements of Writer's Workshop to their K–5 settings. In addition, each participant was asked to bring eight children's books to the institute so that construction of unit plans could directly relate to the grade levels taught in their settings. This helped the teacher-candidates get a sense of appropriate content and connections to the needs of learners in their future internship.

The authors also focused on the critical use of children's literature to support social studies concepts. The participants engaged in critical analysis of typical elementary texts such as *Little House on the Prairie* (Wilder, 1935) and *The Game of Silence* (Erdrich, 2005) to explore the concepts of master- and counter-narratives related to our nation's historical policy toward the removal of Native Americans. They used text analysis protocols such as "The Final Word" (https://www.nsrfharmony.org/wp-content/uploads/2017/10/final_word_0.pdf) to structure these conversations to allow space for challenging personal biases and beliefs.

Participants reported that these hard conversations around personal issues helped them really understand and learn about one another in ways that don't typically happen in the rush of teaching when the school year and internship begin. Therefore, these topics around controversial issues not only leveled the playing field, metaphorically, but they created opportunities for personal connection and understanding to occur.

DESIGN PRINCIPLES FOR SHARED LEARNING EXPERIENCES

In this chapter the authors focused on the design of a shared learning experience prior to internship placement. In their larger study, they did follow the pairs into the first semester of a yearlong internship to examine their mentoring interactions and their relationships. The mentor-intern pairs they studied exhibited the types of mentoring interactions described as educative mentoring (Feiman-Nemser, 2012; Schwille, 2008), which participants connected back to their time spent learning together in the summer (Curcio & Adams, 2019). Based on these findings and the growing literature base on creating and strengthening productive mentor-intern relationships, the authors developed the following design principles for shared learning experiences.

Co-Learners

Mentor-intern pairs connected to institute experiences in which they were situated as learners engaged in new learning. Sometimes these interactions highlighted the strengths of the teacher-candidates and other times the mentor-teachers; nevertheless, these experiences authentically positioned each participant—mentor or teacher-candidate—as a learner.

The participants consistently connected to institute experiences that extended their thinking and provided new knowledge applicable to the classroom. In particular, they noted that structured opportunities for collaborative discussions enabled mentor-intern pairs to bounce ideas off of each other, learn from varied perspectives, and better understand each other's teaching philosophies.

The integration of technology arose as a space in both institutes that situated mentors and teacher candidates as co-learners who learned not only from the institute content, but also from each other. Technology integration occurred as participants identified and shared resources and engaged in the creation of technological products. The ability to explore Web 2.0 tools (e.g., iMovie and Story Jumper) and then use these tools to collaboratively create authentic products provided rich opportunities for co-learning.

These experiences allowed mentor-intern pairs to collectively learn new content, while also discussing its application to the classroom, in a manner that enabled both mentors and interns to draw upon prior knowledge and contribute to learning.

Related to these findings, when studying STEM-oriented shared learning experiences Gunckel and Wood (2016) and Wood and Turner (2015) identified the importance of providing experiences in which both mentors and teacher-candidates can authentically engage as learners. Specifically, Gunckel and Wood (2016) noted the importance of not privileging either mentors or teacher-candidates when designing shared learning experiences. Tasks need to be designed in a manner that allows for all participants to actively contribute to and engage in learning opportunities.

In addition to planning for tasks that authentically situate mentor-intern pairs as co-learners, university-based teacher educators need to consider the facilitation of shared learning experiences to promote productive discourse.

Throughout our institute, protocols were used to structure rich conversations where participants were "forced to be real" and provided opportunities to learn more about each other on personal and professional levels.

The participants referenced various discussion protocols that enabled them to better understand their partner's perceived strengths and areas for growth, and this information contributed to accelerated and strengthened relationships throughout the internship. Similarly, Wood and Turner (2015) discussed the role of university-based teacher educators in facilitating shared learning experiences in a manner that supports co-learning. While Wood and Turner (2015) did not specifically use a discussion protocol, they strategically created tasks that engaged participants in dialogic discourse, and their study noted the importance of the university-based teacher educator as a facilitator who can assist in generating productive third-space conversations aimed at co-learning.

Create Authentic Tasks

Intentionally planning for co-learning entails creating authentic tasks that not only challenge participants' thinking, but also directly apply to the classroom. Well-planned tasks will engage mentor-intern pairs in the creation of shared knowledge, and they should provide a space to value mentor and intern contributions. The participant pairs consistently discussed the importance of the unit plan as an institute task that provided opportunities for productive dialogic discourse regarding the application of institute content within their individual classroom contexts.

Pairs noted how they collaborated to create units that incorporated institute content and pedagogy, while also attending to grade-level standards and their diverse student contexts. In particular, mentor-teachers shared how daily planning facilitated a better understanding of their interns' knowledge and beliefs, and that this insight heightened their sense of trust and productivity upon entering the classroom in the fall.

Writer's Workshop activities focused on citizenship also emerged as influential institute tasks, as mentor-intern pairs engaged in discussions that led to discovering professional and personal similarities and differences. Often these discussions, centered on personal anecdotes, elicited emotions that authentically led to conversations that merged personal and professional beliefs.

Canipe and Gunckel (2019) promoted the inclusion of authentic tasks as boundary objects (Akkerman & Bakker, 2011). Their study, focused on how mentor-intern pairs navigated conversations in co-learning tasks, supporting the need to strategically plan for activities that authentically engage mentor-intern pairs in teaching-related conversations. Ultimately, the authors assert that intentionally planned tasks have the potential to become boundary objects that provide a space in which mentor-teachers and teacher-candidates can negotiate meaning.

Paying Attention to Structures

The participant pairs reported that they were able to get to know one another professionally and personally by spending extended time together. While it is not always feasible or financially possible to create two weeks of learning prior to the internship, their participants definitely needed an extended period of time to learn about one another, including strengths and areas for growth. In addition, the fact that this was held in a neutral location helped communicate that no one began with an advantage or perception of power on their "home field." In terms of third-space concepts, this neutral location did not privilege one discourse over the other, although the authors must acknowledge that power always exists in a graded/supervised experience like an internship.

In addition to location and duration, it is important to note that the shared learning experience they examined took place prior to the internship, not concurrently. Participants reported that this helped them hit the ground running on the first day of class, instead of needing time to get to know and trust one another. The foundation for their mentoring relationship began mid-summer, and often continued informally until school began, although not structured or required by the university.

Turner and Blackburn (2016) supported this issue of timing in their study focused on a shared learning experiences occurring throughout the duration of clinical experiences. Within their study, Turner and Blackburn (2016) noted how co-learning events fostered mentor-intern relationships and advocated for the need to research co-learning events held prior to the onset of clinical experiences. Linking to both timing and duration, the authors also recommend that follow-up occur throughout the year in the form of professional learning for mentor-intern pairs together. These are likely to be day or half-day events, but reconnecting off-site, together with the original summer participants, can support the continued strengthening of mentoring partnerships.

CONCLUSION

The mentor-intern relationship is central to the educative nature of a clinical internship experience; thus, we must explore opportunities to disrupt the traditional mentor-intern hierarchy and strengthen relationship development

(Hudson, 2016). Whereas we recognize that mentors will always hold power within a mentor-intern relationship, we contend that the creation of co-learning experiences prior to the onset of the internship may aid in the development of educative mentor-intern relationships. This chapter focused on a shared learning experience held prior to the clinical internship involving mentor-intern pairs as co-learners.

REFERENCES

Akkerman, S. F., & Bakker, A. (2011). Boundary crossing and boundary objects. *Review of Educational Research, 81* (2), 132–69.

Ambrosetti, A., Knight, B. A., & Dekkers, J. (2014). Maximizing the potential of mentoring: A framework for pre-service teacher education. *Mentoring & Tutoring: Partnership in Learning, 22*(3), 224–39.

American Association of Colleges for Teacher Education. (2018). *A pivot towards clinical practice, its lexicon, and the renewal of educator preparation: A report of the AACTE clinical practice commission.* Washington, DC: Author.

American Association of Colleges for Teacher Education. (2016). *Clinical practice and its lexicon: Toward the renewal of the profession of teaching a pivot toward "clinical practice."* Unpublished manuscript.

Bradbury, L. U., & Koballa, T. R. (2008). Borders to cross: Identifying sources of tension in mentor-intern relationships. *Teaching and Teacher Education, 24*(8), 2132–45.

Bullough, J. R., & Draper, R. J. (2004). Mentoring and the emotions. *Journal of Education for Teaching, 30*(3), 271–88.

Canipe, M. M., & Gunckel, K. L. (2019). Imagination, brokers, and boundary objects: Interrupting mentor-preservice teacher hierarchy when negotiating meanings. *Journal of Teacher Education, 00*(0), 1–14. https://doi.org/10.1177/0022487119840660.

Curcio, R. (2017). *The relationship between attending a shared learning experience and mentoring interactions in the final internship.* (Doctoral dissertation, University of Florida). University of Florida Digital Collection.

Curcio, R., & Adams, A. (2019). The development of mentoring partnerships: How a shared learning experience enhanced the final internship. *SRATE Journal, 28*(1), 1–8.

Darling-Hammond, L., Hammerness, K., Grossman, P., Rust, F., & Shulman, L. (2005). The design of teacher education programs. In L. Darling-Hammond & J. Bransford (Eds.), *Preparing teachers for a changing world: What all teachers should learn to be able to do* (pp. 390–440). San Francisco, CA: Jossey-Bass.

Erdrich, L. (2005). *The game of silence.* New York, NY: Harper-Collins.

Feiman-Nemser, S. (2012). *Teachers as learners.* Cambridge, MA: Harvard Education Press.

Feiman-Nemser, S., & Buchmann, M. (1987). When is student teaching teacher education? *Teaching and Teacher Education, 3*, 255–73.

Flessner, R. (2014). Revisiting reflection: Utilizing third spaces in teacher education. *The Educational Forum, 78*(3,) 231–47.
Gunckel, K. L., & Wood, M. B. (2016). The principle-practical discourse edge: Elementary preservice and mentor teachers working together on co-learning tasks. *Science Teacher Education, 100(*1), 96–121.
Hudson, P. (2016) Forming the mentor-mentee relationship. *Mentoring & Tutoring: Partnership in Learning, 24(*1), 30–43.
National Council for Accreditation of Teacher Education. (2010). *Transforming teacher education through clinical practice: A national strategy to prepare effective educator* [Blue Ribbon Report]. Washington, DC: Author.
Schwille, S. A. (2008). The professional practice of mentoring. *American Journal of Education, 115*(1), 139–67.
Turner, E., & Blackburn, C. (2016). Prospective and mentor teacher perspectives on co-learning events. *Mentoring and Tutoring: Partnership in Learning, 24*(4), 271–89.
Valencia, S. W., Martin, S. D., Place, N. A., & Grossman, P. (2009). Complex interactions in student teaching. *Journal of Teacher Education, 60*(3), 304–22.
Wilder, L. I. (1935). *Little house on the prairie*. New York, NY: Harper & Bros.
Wilson, S., Floden R., & Ferrini-Mundy, S. (2001). *Teacher preparation research: Current knowledge, gaps, and recommendations*. Seattle, WA: Center for the Study of Teaching and Policy.
Wood, M. B., & Turner, E. E. (2015). Bringing the teacher into teacher preparation: Learning from mentor teachers in joint methods activities. *Journal of Math Teacher Education, 18*, 27–51.
Zeichner, K. (2002). Beyond traditional structures of student teaching. *Teacher Education Quarterly, 29*(2), 59–64.
Zeichner, K. (2010). Rethinking the connections between campus courses and field experiences in college- and university-based teacher education. *Journal of Teacher Education, 61*(1–2), 89–99.

Chapter Nine

Realizing Inspiring and Successful Educators (RISE)

A University-School District Partnership to Support Latinx Teacher-Candidates

Sheri Hardee, PhD, and Lauren Johnson, PhD,
University of North Georgia

It is no easy task for community/university partners to create professional development models that truly demonstrate interwoven, mutually beneficial relationships amongst all stakeholders. In particular, it can be difficult to ensure that Educator Preparation Programs (EPPs) collaborate with P–12 partners to provide mutual support for effective clinical coaching and to ensure that candidates are supported during the final clinical internship. The creation of such partnerships is perhaps further complicated when mentor-teachers are not representative of the teacher-candidates and the P–12 students with whom they work.

The U.S. teaching field is primarily comprised of white females (Jupp, Berry, & Lensmire, 2016; Nieto & Bode, 2012), yet this is often not representative of the students with whom these educators work. This is true, for instance, in the school communities with which the authors of this chapter work. As Jupp et al. (2016) noted, we have a "demographic imperative" to ensure that white educators are prepared to work with students from diverse backgrounds and that we are recruiting educators of color (p. 2).

With this in mind, the authors of this chapter developed the Realizing Inspiring and Successful Educators (RISE) program in collaboration with a neighboring school district in an effort to recruit and support Latinx educators. As the current dean and the coordinator of diversity and recruitment initiatives in the College of Education, our goal has been to increase the number of students of color in our programs while also contributing to the teacher workforce in a local school district.

This is a vital demographic on which to focus considering the growth of the Latinx youth population in the United States, the current political climate impacting the P–12 system, and how this climate affects college-going rates within the demographic (Becerra, 2012; Hurtado & Ponjuan, 2005; Pérez, 2017). More importantly, however, our partner school district has a 43 percent Latinx student population and has a vested interest in increasing its number of Latinx, Spanish-speaking educators (Governor's Office of Student Achievement [GOSA], 2017–2018).

The school district seeks to add a Spanish-English bilingual seal to students' diplomas by 2023, and they have realized that more native-Spanish speakers would be needed in the district to accomplish this goal, as only 6 percent of their teaching core is Latinx (GOSA, 2017–2018). The district has also recognized the importance of representation among the teacher workforce for P–12 students. Thus, the university and school district collaborated on a "Grow Your Own" model whereby graduating Latinx high-school students from the district would be recruited into the College of Education of the partnering university.

The school district would pay the students' tuitions and fees in addition to providing paraprofessional positions throughout their four-year college experience; this would ensure that these pre-service educators garner valuable experience and extra funding to assist them in college. These paraprofessional positions would be part of the Educator Preparation Program's (EPP) required field and clinical experiences, and thus university faculty and P–12 teachers would need to work together to craft thoughtful and specialized experiences for RISE participants. In addition, the partnering higher education institution would provide specialized courses for each cohort, academic and career advising, faculty mentors, funding for required certification assessments, and social events each semester to bolster the financial, academic, and social support so vital for student retention.

This chapter explores the development of a foundational model meant to support institutional partnerships seeking to diversify teacher education programs with a specific focus on field and clinical placement development. Through data from a two-year qualitative case study, the authors utilize themes from participant interviews and written reflections to demonstrate how they developed a framework for creating such partnerships and to examine the tension that emerges in liminal spaces—places where the students transition from one border to another.

This includes spaces between the country of origin and the United States, home and P–12 school, P–12 school and college, and home and college. In examining these spaces, the authors explore perceptions of schooling and pedagogical practices voiced by program participants through this project. We also consider how their experiences influenced the continued development of the field and clinical placement model for the RISE program.

The goal here was to examine the experiences of RISE participants, including the obstacles faced and supports needed to transition between these liminal spaces without the need to assimilate to the dominant culture (i.e., white, middle class, monolingual). Understanding these transitional points helped the authors to anticipate related challenges to better prepare teacher-candidates to succeed, especially through communication with their mentor-teachers in their field and clinical placements.

From this study, the authors have a more detailed map outlining how to adapt this specialized teacher education program to meet the needs of and to provide adequate support for students from this particular demographic. While this is not meant to be a one-size-fits-all approach, the authors hope a discussion of this model's development, along with addressing related challenges, will provide a basic framing for others seeking to develop such partnerships. After all, educator preparation programs have a responsibility in teacher education to create models bolstering pre-service educators of color through efforts to support their journeys through college and the induction years of teaching.

THEORETICAL FRAMEWORK

In terms of the theoretical framework, we, the two authors and co-directors of the RISE program, utilized a foundation combining LatCrit, Critical Race, and post-colonial theories enhanced by scholarship more specifically focused on social justice education and pedagogy. As we reviewed relevant literature and listened to our students' stories about attending and working in our partner schools, we recognized the macro and micro impacts of racism in their lives, the influence of the past and the present on these experiences, and, in particular, how bias manifested in their K–16 educational experiences, including their current work in their paraprofessional positions (Solórzano & Yosso, 2001a).

LatCrit theories allow the researchers to expand the reach of Critical Race Theory (CRT) to "reveal the ways Latinas/os experience race, class, gender, and sexuality, while also acknowledging the Latina/o experience with issues of immigration status, language, ethnicity and culture" (Pérez Huber, 2010, p. 79). These intersections also provide a means for exploring "racist nativism," which "continues to exclude Latinas/os who are perceived to be undocumented Mexican immigrants" (Pérez Huber, 2010, p. 81).

As Solórzano and Yosso argued, the combination of CRT and LatCrit theories offers a means for examining racism, oppression, and power and can provide powerful mechanisms for deconstructing and dismantling oppressive forces through counternarratives or counter-storytelling. As Solórzano & Yosso (2001b) noted, "a critical race and LatCrit methodology offers a way to understand students' experiences with such concepts as self-doubt, survivor guilt, impostor syndrome, and invisibility. A critical race methodology generates knowledge by looking to those who have been epistemologically marginalized, silenced, and disempowered" (p. 488). In particular, many LatCrit scholars have argued for the need for spaces where Latinx students can dialogue, critique dominant ideologies, and build strength with one another to then move into spaces where this dismantling can occur (Diaz Soto, Cervantes-Soon, Villarreal, & Campos, 2009).

We see our RISE students and those Latinx students in our partner schools as needing empowering spaces in both P–16 education settings and within the space of teacher education. Given both the historical background and the current climate surrounding immigration in our country, our framing became rooted in Paulo Freire's (2000) conscientization, or critical awareness of one's social reality through empowering education. The question then centered on where this empowering education would occur when traditional banking models dominate the P–16 setting. The banking model, as coined by Freire (2000), highlighted the danger of traditional models of education whereby students are not challenged to think critically but are encouraged to be mere receptacles of knowledge.

This knowledge, however, is too often steeped in dominant ideologies, thus reinforcing stereotypes and systemic oppression. Thus, we expanded on our conceptual framing utilizing postcolonial theories and the concept of the physical and metaphorical borderland. Many of our participants have had the literal experience of crossing a border into an environment that is unwelcoming at best. Through their schooling and social experiences, they have experienced a metaphorical border as well: They are not accepted into the dominant culture at the same time they are expected to attempt to assimilate. This creates a cultural division that leaves students in a specific type of liminal space.

Borderlands are not easy places in which to exist. As Anzaldúa (1999) described, they are fraught with tension, yet they can provide a place for self- and community exploration. We want to provide our RISE students with spaces for communal strength where they can gain the tools necessary to deconstruct dominant culture rather than assimilate to it. We want them to build the confidence to share their stories and cultures in these spaces, and this is particularly important in that our Latinx educators will be able to provide those sacred spaces for their Latinx students (Diaz Soto et al., 2009).

As educators and researchers who are not Latinx, we can facilitate our students' exploration of the need for these spaces at the same time we remain outside of the realm of their experiences. The hope is that RISE participants are able to create those protected spaces to explore racist nativism, oppression, and power from similar perspectives to those of their students. While we recognize that college is not typically this space, we hope the structures and supports we offer can provide metaphorical spaces within the oppressive confines of higher education.

Additionally, the authors want their P–12 partners to understand the need for such spaces within their settings. As Haddix (2017) suggested, "It is also important that we critically examine the policies and practices that impede goals of teacher diversity. This critique can only happen when teacher education programs leverage the voices and experiences of current teachers of color and students of color" (p. 147). This is a particularly important step for enhancing field and clinical experiences and should be integrated, as we will discuss below, into clinical training for mentor-teachers and supervisors.

Such critical examination of educator preparation, from the university classroom to the clinical experiences, requires participation from our RISE students, their teacher education peers, their faculty, and our partner schools. As noted, social justice education cannot start at the level of teacher education programs; rather, it should be all-encompassing. Even for our teacher education students placed in diverse settings, these experiences often serve only to reify stereotypes if not carefully constructed and combined with appropriate theories and pedagogies.

This job can be made more difficult by the fact that many teacher education students and their P–12 mentors enter these environments with monocultural viewpoints and demonstrate resistance to discussions of diversity (Beilke, 2005; Butin 2005; Sensoy & DiAngelo, 2012). This is why carefully structured courses and assignments are key. In Social Foundations courses designed for RISE cohorts, students are provided pedagogical strategies and readings to assist with their work as paraprofessionals, and specifically for their work with English Language Learners (ELLs).

Course readings are centered on the experiences of students of color in schools from a social justice perspective including issues of immigration, language acquisition, culturally relevant pedagogy, and race/racism. Students in these courses are encouraged to make connections between their experiences as Latinx students in predominantly white school settings and the experiences of the current students they work with as paraprofessionals in the same school district.

RESEARCH METHODS AND PROGRAM BACKGROUND

This project originated after a College of Education Advisory Board Council meeting, during which time our partner district for this project noted that their goal was to offer students a bilingual seal on their diplomas by 2023. However, they did not have the number of heritage Spanish speakers necessary to fulfill this goal. The district also recognized the importance of representation for Latinx P–12 students—they realized that increasing the number of Latinx educators could help engage Latinx students in their education and hiring heritage Spanish speakers could place increased value on Spanish as the L1 (first language learned) for students entering school with Spanish as their first language, thus increasing the potential for academic success by approaching bilingual education from an additive perspective (Nieto & Bode, 2012). Upon hearing this, we jointly developed a Grow Your Own model whereby we would recruit Latinx graduates from the district's high schools into our College of Education. The district would pay their tuition and books, while the college would provide additional academic, social, and financial supports.

While they are in college, these students would be hired as part-time paraprofessionals into the same school district. These paraprofessional positions would serve as students' field and clinical experiences; a mentor-teacher and university supervisor would supervise each student. The RISE program requires a special type of partnership in relation to field and clinical experiences. These experiences differ from traditional Educator Preparation Program (EPP) placements for students in length, and, as paid positions, they necessitate stronger relationships with principals and mentor-teachers to ensure that both the needs of the school and the college requirements were being met.

These experiences also demand that stakeholders be in constant communication regarding RISE participants and P–12 students. To provide additional support, the program includes a summer orientation for RISE students, faculty mentors, and individualized advising, mid-semester progress reports from instructors, social events throughout the year, and cohort-specific sections of education courses starting from day one. To provide additional comparison and context here, students in our traditional EPPs do not begin their education courses or field experiences until the junior year.

This qualitative case study includes two years of data highlighting the experiences of twenty-three program participants, all of whom are first-generation college students between eighteen to twenty-four years old. Data for the project included students' written work, two surveys, one focus group, and individual participant interviews. We sought to address the following questions:

1. What are the issues for Latinx youth in K–12 schools? How do school cultures in Georgia contribute to these issues?
2. How could teachers from similar backgrounds/communities assist in developing effective supports for Latinx students?
3. How can universities/colleges of education develop partnerships with communities and schools to increase the number of Latinx educators?
4. What supports and resources are needed in the process?

The authors initially analyzed our data using conventional content analysis, and we employed in-vivo coding (Saldaña, 2013) to capture specific words or phrases directly from the students that illustrated categories or patterns. In looking for patterns, we highlighted instances of causation and correspondence, so we were asking our students to tell their stories and then following up with questions that required them to reflect on how these events made them feel or what triggered a particular feeling or action.

The authors encouraged students to describe their transitions to college and their participation in the RISE program, including reflections on their work as paraprofessionals in their home county schools as compared to their prior experiences as students in the district. Emergent themes from students' counternarratives included the tension created by the impact of immigration on students and their families and the tension that results from a pull between the family culture and "American culture" (i.e., white, middle class–dominant culture and the tension resulting from families' complex views on education). Additionally, participants related their motivations as educators and how these have been influenced by their work as paraprofessionals and by their coursework in the College of Education. This included emphasis on supports provided by mentor-teachers and university faculty and areas for improvement in relation to these roles. In the findings, the authors present the themes mentioned above and then provide a discussion as to the direct impact of these themes on field and clinical placement, including development provided to clinical educators.

FINDINGS

RISE program participants interviewed and surveyed for this study shared similar tensions with respect to their experiences as first- or second-generation immigrants and the ways in which their schooling was shaped by issues of immigration, culture, and family. These students have had the experiences of being undocumented and DACA-mented, they have parents and other family members who have gone through status changes, and national and statewide immigration policy changes have affected them directly and indirectly.

For some, this has meant the challenge of managing academic work and employment with the compounded stress of potential deportation for themselves or their loved ones. They learned to separate their home and school lives, keeping academic struggles at school and their family pressures and responsibilities at home. There were multiple ways in which their experiences in P–12 schools in the United States, and Georgia in particular, were incongruous with their home cultures.

Issues of exclusion were salient for a number of students who described the lack of communication between their schools and parents, their parents' inability to assist them with schoolwork, and restrictions placed on them by teachers and administrators who emphasized "English only" policies. Finally, multiple students expressed in interviews and written reflections that they struggle to meet their parents' expectations regarding work and academic success. For many RISE students, they are achieving their parents' dreams by attending college and studying to become educators. As one RISE student stated, "My parents immigrated here so, like, we can have a better life, not just so we can graduate high school and go get a job like they did. No, it's like, 'Go get that certification so you don't have to work as hard as I did.'" For others, focusing on a degree rather than full-time employment is a sacrifice for families in need of additional income.

Due to the focus in program-specific Social Foundations courses on RISE students' work as paraprofessionals, we found it pertinent to explore connections students made between their daily experiences in K–8 classrooms as paraprofessionals, their previous experiences as students, and course preparation. For RISE students just beginning their college journeys, a quick transition is required from the role of high school student to that of a professional working with children.

Data collected for this project indicated that many students find that the teachers and administrators where they now work differ significantly from those who impacted their own schooling. As one participant wrote:

> The staff and faculty at [elementary school] really care about the students. I feel like I have never been in a school where everyone understands the different backgrounds we are coming from and how important it is to care for the student's culture and language. The teachers at this school will not judge you for speaking Spanish; instead they want to learn more to be able to communicate better with the students. [. . .] The school even has free English classes for the parents of the students so that they can communicate and help their children with homework. The school overall feels like home, and that's how every school for every student should feel like.

In fact, several participants highlighted the importance of this feeling of community at the schools in which they work.

When asked what she liked about working in the partner district, one student noted, "Um, like in my school particularly, I love the community. Like, you can tell that it's a closer community. Um, there's a lot of parents who are willing to help. Even for teacher appreciation week we had such a good turnout, like they brought us in so much food." Another participant echoed, "I kind of like being in a familiar place, in familiar people, faces and teachers so I really like being back with family." These were not the only instances in which participants utilized the terms *family* and *home* in referring to their placements and the sense of community within their schools.

In part, this sense of community likely stems from participants becoming paraprofessionals in schools and working with teachers with whom they interacted as P–12 students. This sense of community is likely further enhanced by a shared cultural community, and, as noted in the quotation above, a dedication on behalf of the mentor-teachers and district to incorporate the community and culture into the school environment.

In terms of the participants' backgrounds, nearly all participants have suggested in interviews or written reflections that they relate to the students they currently work with due to similar linguistic and cultural knowledge and experiences as P–12 students in the district. A participant described how she related to the students in the following statement:

> Well, okay, so I have kids not only from Mexico. I have some from El Salvador that, like, I can relate to them. I have some from El Salvador. I have two from Colombia and Cuba, and I think one from Puerto Rico. So, like, I listen to them and talk to them about their families and stuff, and I think it's so interesting to know where they came from and some of them, they're first-generation.

Having similar experiences, this student has been able to relate to her students in a way that even her mentor-teacher has not been able to manage. Yet their teachers also encourage intercultural community in the classroom. As another participant noted of her mentor-teacher:

> ... she is very open to culture actually. So, we read this poem about this, um, it wasn't in Spanish, but it was, like, about, like, Spanish stuff, and it just had, like, words like *leche* and *tamal*, and for her to teach a poem like that ... I was like, she is teaching to her audience, she is teaching to, like, she could have picked a poem by like Edgar Allen Poe or like ... that's amazing, yeah, because you, you don't, I feel like that's something we need more of ...

Indeed, through class discussions on topics relating to the sociocultural issues that students face, our students demonstrate crucial connections between the cultural, linguistic, economic, and political issues that impact our education system and the daily lives of children.

From these readings, discussions, and their accompanying field experiences, RISE participants also explore the limitations placed on Latinx students in U.S. schools. In terms of readings, articles that analyze the barriers to inclusion for Latinx youth in schools convey the significance of social justice pedagogy for participants who have rarely been exposed to readings on the oppression of their specific cultural group in our society (Blanchard & Muller, 2015; Irizarry, 2015; Marx & Larson, 2012; Sanchez, 2016). As one participant described:

> One way that I would allow these readings to influence my decisions in my classroom is by looking at the eye-opening stories and backgrounds of my students. Each one of them has a story to tell, and it is my job to listen or learn to listen to them. By exploring their cultures, I can see what they like to do, how they may think, and I can use that information to make classroom-based decisions. Making them not feel inferior to any other race is a goal of mine because sometimes they feel like that, and that does not allow them to be confident and pursue things they are capable of doing. The United States is coming around; from encouraging bilingual instruction, to banning foreign languages at an attempt to "Americanize" immigrants, to foreign languages being taught in school and multicultural classes existing and creating a positive impact on the kids.

In these courses, students engage research on the educational experiences of Latinx youth in the United States in ways that they did not during their P–12 schooling. They participate in the construction of knowledge in their college classes, questioning and criticizing the work of scholars that, at times, confirms their perceptions and, at others, opposes their own narratives about schooling and its effects.

The responses of RISE participants to this course content seem to indicate a sense of empowerment and efficacy that comes with the desire to act as a change agent in one's community. A RISE student in her first year at UNG wrote:

> I have learned that there is not an easy way to helping [sic] every student but there are resources that can be used to push the child into the right direction. I am able to see the struggles that students go through when they do not have someone to help them due to language barriers. When I was in elementary school this was one of the issues that I had because my parents did not know English and there was no one at home to help me. I want to be able to help all the students I can who go through things like this.

As these pre-service teachers increase their knowledge of pedagogical strategies and ways to assist their mentor-teachers in classrooms, they are encouraged to be the leaders that they needed as students.

This includes consideration of the challenges they faced in P–12 classrooms, the methods and approaches of their previous teachers, both effective and ineffective, and the types of learning environments that surrounded them in schools and at home. RISE participants demonstrate the understanding that the deficits some of their teachers and administrators perceived in them were the exact assets that currently motivate them to become educators. The following quotation is from a second-year participant:

> Latino students feel *cero a la izquierda*, which means they do not count. "'I want teachers to teach me like they want me to go to the best college, how they would want teachers to teach their kids'—Taína" [Irizarry, 2015, p. 68]. Educators believe that Latino students are not capable of handling challenging and interesting learning opportunities. As a future Latino educator this does make an impact. No one should feel *cero a la izquierda*. Everyone should have an opportunity no matter who they are.

While part of this empowerment comes from the content and discussions in which they are engaging with their faculty in classes, the other half comes from their field and clinical experiences and the manner in which they interact with their mentor-teachers. Overwhelmingly, the participants noted that their mentor-teachers were affirming, understanding, and worked to ensure that the RISE participants were engaged in their experiences. As one student noted of her paraprofessional experience with her mentor-teacher:

> When I first got there, I thought that I was gonna be the parapro . . . okay, she [mentor-teacher] was gonna go send me to print out everything, pass out papers, like do many things in class, but she's not like that. She is very open to what I have to say about the classroom and how we can improve and if I would like to teach lessons, and like, she's not demanding of me, like, to do certain things, but she's always open to my opinion.

This student entered her field experience believing that she would be participating more logistically or in an administrative assistant manner, but she was surprised to find that her mentor-teacher cared about her opinions and worked to integrate her into the class as a co-educator. Similarly, another participant sharing a paraprofessional position with another RISE student noted the following about her experience with her mentor-teacher:

> If we had a question, she always helped us, or she [mentor-teacher] directed us [to] somebody that could help us and she let us do a lot of our own stuff like working with the kids. She wasn't, she didn't want it to be one certain way, so she let us do a lot of our own things.

The students were surprised at the level of authority and control their mentor-teachers extended to them in the classroom, and the majority indicated that their mentor-teachers encouraged participation and creative thought. Another participant made a significant connection when she relayed the following about her experience with her mentor-teacher:

> Um, she kind of reminded me of my mom a little bit and so it was kind of like, oh my goodness, like, my mom is super strict but then she can be really lovey-dovey with the kids and myself sometimes, but then she'd make me do some ridiculous chores and, anyways, but it was just over, I learned a lot from her, and at times I was just like, maybe you could do this to change it up. So, we both gave advice on how we could really improve this different in her classroom and my future classroom, so it was really nice to have that connection and that feedback with her.

In part, the authors hope that these positive relationships are a direct result of the training and communication that occurs between the university and the community partners. In comparison with our traditional educator preparation programs, the RISE program presents a unique situation because students are both employees of the school district and students, meaning they have course requirements to be completed within field and clinical placements. Both parties, the P–12 school and the university faculty, have to be clear about expectations for each role because we do not want to place the students in another situation in which they feel pulled between two roles: professional and student.

For new students, both the university and the school district train them on professional expectations over the summer. Participating schools, principals, and teachers are hand-selected by the district's human resources to ensure a positive yet challenging experience for RISE participants, and all school partners are well-versed on the program, including the goals and expectations. The university trains mentor-teachers, as well, via online modules.

This training covers expectations for course assignments, goals for co-teaching, dispositional and professional issues, and norming for assessments utilized by the Educator Preparation Program (EPP) to evaluate students. In terms of dispositions, pedagogy, and content, all students self-evaluate utilizing two state-developed instruments, and mentor-teachers and university supervisors evaluate them every semester.

The student, mentor-teacher, and university supervisor meet regularly to discuss strengths and areas for improvement, and university faculty visit students and the school once per week to ensure that these lines of communication remain open. Additionally, the EPP develops a memorandum of understanding with each school partner, outlining the requirements for mentor-teachers and the roles of both the partner school and the university in meeting all students' needs.

DISCUSSION AND IMPLICATIONS

The level of communication described above, though, does not mean that challenges do not exist. One aspect that the students have recognized about their placement schools is that resources, especially for bilingual students, are scarce, and their teachers often seem "overwhelmed" and "overloaded," two terms participants commonly used in the interviews. Every participant interviewed noted that one resource lacking in the county was bilingual educators, and this scarcity impacts the education being provided to the P–12 students and their families.

In watching her mentor-teacher struggle with middle-grades classroom management, one participant relayed the following sentiment to her interviewee (another RISE participant and student researcher):

> Student: The teacher I work with, um, she's like, "You guys do your homework, finish up your essay or I'm gonna be emailing your parents." Like, you can email these parents all you want, or do they even have an email address? You can email them in English, but they won't be read, you know?
>
> Interviewee: So, did the students just kinda, like, laugh when she says that because they know that unfortunately their parents are unable to read the emails or the notes she sends them home?
>
> Student: Yeah exactly.
>
> Interviewee: So, I think it would really help if they were able to send them or type emails in Spanish or text them—I mean, yeah, text them or write in their agendas in Spanish.
>
> Student: Or contact their home like, "*Hola, Señora.*"

The RISE participants, in most cases, end up as the only bilingual employees in their school settings. Almost every participant interviewed indicated that a major facet of their roles as paraprofessionals involved translating and working with students with Spanish as their L1 and their families.

While participants noted that this was a challenging role to be in, they also appreciated the experience it provided them and the results they saw from their efforts:

> One of my classes was just a really struggle bus. So, they were all Hispanic, and I had to translate some, and at the end of the year, one of my students wrote

me a little note saying, like, "Oh, wow, like, you made me really wanna push myself." And I was like, "Don't make me start crying." But, you know, it's just like, as long as you change one kid, as you really reach that with either the material or with the lesson, the life lesson, you're doing a great job. So, being with them made me realize, this is who I am, this is what I wanna do, this is what I wanna become.

Additionally, we have learned that while welcoming and inclusive in terms of teaching, some of our mentor-teachers still hold biases that impact their RISE paraprofessionals. One participant, for instance, stated that while her mentor-teacher liked her, she was often biased against the students of color in her classroom: "There's some things she says to the students that I'm like . . . I don't think we're supposed to say that." This same participant then relayed the following story:

> She [the mentor-teacher] once said something that really like hit me, and I was like, "What?" She's like, she said, we were talking about the border wall, so like, um, how some kids, 'cause they're Hispanic so they're like obviously not gonna want it and their parents are Mexican or whatever . . . And she's like, "If you lock your doors at night, then you want a wall." She said, like, "If you lock your doors at night, you want a wall." . . . Yeah, and she said to like to 13–14-year-olds and was like . . . yeah, and then she looked at me and she's like, "Am I right?" Then I'm like, uh, I don't want to voice my opinions because mine are completely different from yours.

In this particular situation, the RISE student felt pulled as a professional between agreeing with her teacher and remaining silent, and she chose the latter. Again, this highlights the tension that many RISE participants feel in the classroom when such instances occur.

What we have learned is that research too often fails to examine assets of Latinx youth, particularly how they creatively navigate the obstacles and issues thrown in front of them, and more counter-stories highlighting that these journeys are needed. Additionally, more training is needed with our school partners in preparation for field and clinical experiences to ensure that culturally relevant pedagogies and culturally sensitive practices and approaches are being employed.

In particular, EPPs need additional work examining these borderland, or *encuentro*, spaces that provide a place for youth to examine and gain critical literacies for dismantling dominant ideologies. We should work to ensure that our mentor-teachers and clinical educators understand the need for and how to create such spaces for their college and P–12 students. Too often there is not a language for discussing documentation at school; too often Latinx youth are placed in the position of acting as a "go between" between parents, teachers, and administrators; and too often language is not provided the emphasis that it needs (from an additive perspective).

After all, language is empowerment, and it is important for Latinx children/youth to have spaces where the language of children/youth and the LI are prioritized, and dialogic encounters can occur. This was made evident to us, as authors and researchers, through our work with this program. One of our students summed this up best when she highlighted the link between her own schooling experiences and her goals as a future educator and current paraprofessional:

> Like, I kinda wish my teacher would've been able to, like, kind of get me. So, I guess that's what I want to get them [P–12 students] to experience, like, since I know Spanish, I can get someone in Spanish. And it's kind of like I don't have to be like, "Oh, you have to go do a different assignment, get to get out of the class." I kind of want to teach them in there, teach everyone, you get it?

We value that the RISE participants "get" their students, but we want their mentor-teachers and schools to recognize the importance of this as well.

This means we have to continue to work to build the types of relationships in which we can have difficult discussions regarding bias, oppression, power, and privilege. With this in mind, we, the co-coordinators and authors of this chapter, have recommended that the program begin to incorporate regular meetings between us and the district's participating personnel so that we can all discuss measures for mutually beneficial and collaborative professional development.

What we have learned through this experience is that in terms of partnerships in such projects, these have to be navigated with care, but researchers also have to be willing to step in and speak when needed. We, as researchers, have learned that we must diplomatically engage in critique in an effort to maintain relationships at the same time that we push back against oppressive policies and approaches.

It cannot be expected that our mentor-teachers and the partners with whom we work have the understanding and awareness needed to effectively mentor future Latinx educators in a manner that encourages social justice and social action. This is where careful relationships, trust building, and training are key—the school spaces belong to the teachers, administrators, and their students, and as partners and outsiders, we need their support and willingness to engage.

This is why a strong foundation in CRT, LatCrit, and postcolonial theories is vital from the outset to ensure that such relationships can be created. As we develop partnerships, it is imperative to bring in all voices and ensure that we examine every aspect of the project from multiple and intersecting identities.

REFERENCES

Anzaldúa, G. E. (1999). *Borderlands/La frontera: The new Mestiza*. San Francisco, CA: Aunt Lute Books.

Becerra, D. (2012). Perceptions of educational barriers affecting the academic achievement of Latino K–12 students. *Children & Schools, 34*(3), 167–77.

Beilke, J. R. (2005). Whose world is this? *Multicultural Education, 12*(3), 2–7.

Blanchard, S., & Muller, C. (2015). Gatekeepers of the American dream: How teachers' perceptions shape the academic outcomes of immigrant and language-minority students. *Social Science Research, 51*, 262–75.

Butin, D.W. (2005). Identity (re)construction and student resistance. In D.W. Butin (Ed.), *Teaching social foundations of education: Contexts, theories, and issues*, (pp. 109–26). Mahway, NJ: Lawrence Erlbaum Associates, Inc.

Diaz Soto, L., Cervantes-Soon, C., Villarreal, E., & Campos, E. (2009). The Xicana sacred space: A communal circle of compromiso for educational researchers. *Harvard Educational Review, 79*(4), 755–76.

Freire, P. (2000). *Pedagogy of the oppressed* (30th Anniversary Ed.). New York, NY: Continuum Books.

Georgia Department of Education. (2016). *Enrollment by ethnicity/race, gender and grade level (PK–12)*. Retrieved from https://app3.doe.k12.ga.us/ows-bin/owa/fte_pack_ethnicsex.entry_form.

Governor's Office of Student Achievement (n.d.). Report Card 2017–2018. Retrieved from https://gosa.georgia.gov/report-card-dashboards-data/report-card.

Haddix, M. M. (2017). Diversifying teaching and teacher education: Beyond rhetoric and toward real change. *Journal of Literacy Research, 49*(1), 141–49.

Hurtado, S., & Ponjuan, L. (2005). Latino educational outcomes and the campus climate. *Journal of Hispanic Higher Education, 4*(3), 235–51.

Irizarry, J. G. (2015). What Latino students want from school. *Educational Leadership, 72*(6), 66–71.

Jupp, J., Berry, T. R., & Lensmire, T. (2016). Second wave white teacher identity studies: A review of white teacher identity literature from 2004 through 2014. *Review of Educational Research, 20*(10), 1–41.

Marx, S., & Larson, L. L. (2012). Taking off the color-blind glasses: Recognizing and supporting Latino/a students in a predominantly white school. *Education Administrative Quarterly, 48*, 259–303.

Nieto, S., & Bode, P. (2012) *Affirming diversity: The sociopolitical context of multicultural education* (6th ed.). Boston, MA: Pearson.

Pérez Huber, L. (2010). Using Latino/a critical race theory (LatCrit) and racist nativism to explore intersectionality in the educational experiences of undocumented Chicana college students. *Educational Foundations, 24*(1–2), 77–96.

Pérez, W. (2017). *Americans by heart: Undocumented Latino students and the promise of higher education*. New York, NY: Teachers College Press.

Saldaña, J. (2016). *The coding manual for qualitative researchers* (3rd ed.). Thousand Oaks, CA: SAGE Publications.

Sanchez, C. (April 11, 2016). *Gifted, but still learning English, many bright students get overlooked.* Retrieved from https://www.npr.org/sections/ed/2016/04/11/467653193/gifted-but-still-learning-english-overlooked-underserved.

Sensoy, Ö., & DiAngelo, R. (2012). *Is everyone really equal? An introduction to key concepts in social justice education.* New York, NY: Teachers College.

Solórzano, D. G., & Yosso, T. J. (2001a). From racial stereotyping and deficit discourse toward a critical race theory in education. *Multicultural Education, 9*(1), 2–8.

Solórzano, D. G., & Yosso, T. J. (2001b). Critical race and LatCrit theory and method: Counter-storytelling. *Qualitative Studies in Education, 14*(4), 471–795.

Chapter Ten

Searching for Partnerships to Transform Clinical Practice Experiences

A Case Study

Blake West, EdD, National Education Association

Student learning may be more profoundly impacted by the quality of the teacher than any other school-based factor (Coleman et al., 1966). To ensure every student has access to a competent and caring teacher, the National Education Association (NEA) has a rich history of efforts to strengthen teacher preparation (e.g., co-founding the National Council for Accreditation of Teacher Education [NCATE] in 1954) and offering extensive professional growth for educators.

In 2010–2011, NEA's assembled a task force of exemplary educators to chart a challenging vision for the future of the teaching profession. Their report, *Transforming Teaching: Connecting Professional Responsibility with Student Learning* (NEA, 2011), serves as the basis for NEA's continued work to lead the profession.

The goal that each new teacher is "profession-ready" from the outset of her/his career is crucial to achieving equitable access to a quality education for each student. High-quality extended clinical internship before a teacher-candidate becomes the teacher of record is a powerful strategy to achieve NEA's vision. The knowledge, skills, and dispositions of the mentor-teacher both as a P–12 educator and as an instructional coach and mentor form the basis for the quality of clinical experiences (CCSSO, 2012; AACTE, 2018).

NEA's 2011 report stated, "We envision a system in which candidates acquire this knowledge and learn these skills through significant school-based experiences" (p. 10). The report delineated content and pedagogical knowledge and skills that should be acquired as part of school-based experiences. It also noted in its description of teacher instructional leadership the necessity of the role of "new teacher developer" (NEA, 2011, p. 14). However, there is a lack of consistent processes to select, prepare, and support these mentor-teachers (Hall, Hughes, & Thelk, 2017; NCATE, 2010; Ross, 2002).

Grounded in the 2011 task force recommendations, the Teacher Quality department of NEA's Center for Great Public Schools embarked on a multi-year project in 2012 to develop training and supports for mentor-teachers. NEA enlisted a design team of exemplary educators including higher education faculty, experienced P–12 educators, researchers, and teacher-candidates still engaged in the preparation process. Many of the P–12 and higher education design team members in this project were also familiar with a wide range of preparation program models through extensive service as site visitors, program reviewers, or accreditation board/panel members.

In addition to development of a curriculum for preparing mentor-teachers, the design team experts outlined a variety of delivery models, from an abbreviated one-day workshop, an intensive two-day event, and a semester-long ongoing "course." Common to all models was a partnership between an NEA local affiliate and an Educator Preparation Provider (EPP).

DESIGN PRINCIPLES

Even as a curriculum and delivery models for professional growth of teacher-mentors were being developed in 2015, NEA undertook to answer an overarching question: What does it take to support a teacher's professional learning from recruitment through retirement?

An expert panel was convened in 2016 and released its landmark report in 2017, including a vision of what professional learning should be like for teacher-candidates and for mentor-teachers. The report describes mentor-teachers as:

> skillful teachers, demonstrating accomplished practice, and are carefully matched with candidates. They participate in ongoing professional development to enhance their skills as teachers and as mentors of future teachers. They model a commitment to continuous learning that strengthens professional practice and deepens their understanding of self, along with the culture and backgrounds of their students, colleagues, and communities. (NEA, 2017, p. 15)

CURRICULUM FRAMEWORK

Adult Learning

Principles of adult learning are central to the curriculum and experiences for mentor-teachers. Mentor-teachers must also understand these principles to work effectively with teacher-candidates (Knowles, 1973). Professional learning grounded in understanding adult learners is enhanced through collaboration and contributes to both retention and growth of educators and impacts the culture that adults create for students in their classrooms (Papay & Kraft, 2017). Creating an atmosphere for all learners, particularly adults, requires opportunities for autonomy, development of mastery, and tapping in to the mentor-teacher's sense of purpose (Pink, 2009).

Communication Skills

Communications skills for mentoring are foundational to establishing relationships and providing meaningful support and coaching for teacher-candidates (Knight, 2011). Communication skills must include listening skills, and both verbal and nonverbal communication skills. Active listeners reflect understanding, ask thoughtful questions, and display genuine interest. Mentor-teachers are encouraged to embrace the goal of seeking first to understand.

Difficult Conversations

Communication at times means conveying feedback that may be difficult to hear or presenting new ideas that challenge a teacher-candidate's previous frames of reference. Crucial conversations are defined as stakes are high, emotions run deep, and parties may not be in agreement (Patterson, Grenny, McMillan, & Switzler, 2012). Techniques for monitoring both the body language of others and to be aware of one's own physiological signs of stress are an essential tool to facilitate creating a safe place for difficult conversations. Often, objective tools for observation provide a vehicle for entering into a difficult conversation with a spirit of support rather than judgment (Lipton & Wellman, 2018).

Equity Literacy

Pre-service teachers generally enter teacher preparation programs with minimal cross-cultural experiences. Preparation programs often introduce teacher-candidates to concepts of cultural awareness through curriculum and even early field experiences working with diverse students. But it is still common for teacher-candidates to lack a sense of their own cultural lens and how personal experiences affect their beliefs and biases (Peters, Margolin, Fragnoli, & Bloom, 2016). Mentor-teachers must challenge inequities as well as create and model socially just learning environments (NEA, 2018). Mentor-teachers learn of the needs for teacher-candidates to experience culturally responsive practices, as well (Osler, 2016).

Feedback and Coaching

Providing feedback and coaching are extensions of communications skills and may require ability to engage in difficult conversations. Coaching skills also require fluency with a broad range of pedagogical options, being familiar with individual student needs and abilities, and being able to foster a trusting relationship with the teacher-candidate. A mentor-teacher must understand how to collect and objectively utilize meaningful observation data. Just as the type and extent of teaching activities engaged in by the teacher-candidate grow in magnitude and complexity over time, the ability to rely increasingly on the facilitated reflective conversation grows. Discerning how to make judgments and when to provide feedback is an essential skill for mentor-teachers (Hall, Hughes, & Thelk, 2017). In addition to role-playing and use of video to explore effective coaching conversations, examples of data collection and feedback tools are provided (Killion & Harrison, 2017; Knight, 2011; Knight, 2018; Lipton & Wellman, 2018).

Positive Professional Relationships

Informal feedback provided to the curriculum development team members by experienced mentor-teachers included a consistent message. While some EPPs provide orientation and ongoing engagement between the program, the candidate, and the mentor-teacher, many do not. Vignettes based on the experiences of the curriculum team reveal a need for the mentor-teacher to initiate conversations with the EPP to clarify roles, schedules, evaluation practices, etc.

Mentor-teachers use example scenarios of initial meetings and relationship-building with teacher-candidates to develop scripts for what they might do (Killion & Harrison, 2017; Knight, 2018). There is an emphasis on establishing professional expectations that align with the norms for the placement site. The mentor-teacher also models professionalism as a lifelong learner who is also engaged in professional learning and utilizing goal setting (e.g., SMART goals) to provide focus and chart growth.

Teaching about Teaching

Conversations about pedagogy will vary based on the emphasis of the EPP and the past experiences of the student-teacher. Still, a strong focus on active participation, relevant curriculum, and authentic demonstrations of learning are part of NEA's vision for classrooms and opportunities for student learning (NEA, 2017). Following the publication of the Model Code of Ethics for Educators by the National Association of State Directors of Teacher Education and Certification, the curriculum was expanded to include vignettes representing ethical dilemmas for educators. Mentor-teachers reflect on their own professional experience and setting to anticipate opportunities to engage teacher-candidates in discussions of ethics. They also are encouraged to model how professionals develop confidential collaborative relationships with key school personnel to provide additional insights and perspectives when questions arise for which a clear right-or-wrong answer is not evident.

METHOD

It should be noted that this initiative to provide professional growth opportunities and support to mentor-teachers was not a designed research project. It is offered as a retrospective case study for reflection on both project design and implementation.

The plan for implementation of pilots with NEA's curriculum was grounded in the importance of engaging partners from higher education (AACTE, 2018) and/or from school districts. Partners must also be able to customize the program to meet local needs and the developmental needs of teacher-candidates. The curriculum was purposefully designed so that partners would utilize, adapt, add, and cut in order to make the program their own. NEA recognized that the autonomy for local design and expertise among the partners was congruent with principles of human motivation (Pink, 2009) crucial to enthusiastic participation and would be to the benefit of all participants.

Even without partners readily available in fall 2015, NEA also recognized the demand to make supports available to members where neither district nor EPP offered resources. NEA recognized that additional options for delivery were both feasible and might help to meet a pressing need. The following provides brief descriptions of delivery options NEA employed.

Model A—Workshop Implementation

EPP partnerships. NEA presented its initiative during a session at CAEPCon in September 2015. The weekend seminar and typical semester course were two delivery models shared with attendees. Utilizing a partnership between NEA and an EPP would help to ensure that mentor-teachers would receive desired support, that coaching offered by mentor-teachers would be congruent with expectations of the EPP, and that feedback to teacher-candidates would be aligned with any EPP-required assessment instruments.

State partnership. A second model for implementation emerged as an outgrowth of the 2015 CAEPCon presentation. Interested EPPs approached a state department of education to determine if NEA's curriculum and delivery might meet new state policies for preparation of cooperating teachers. Favorable response from the state department of education led to a two-day workshop training for potential district and EPP trainers of mentor-teachers. If taken to scale, this implementation might make it possible for EPPs without a current training for mentor-teachers to utilize the state model.

Model B—Micro-Credentials

Micro-credentials (MC) provide individuals with access to professional development even when it is not available from an EPP and when no partnership has been established. NEA investigated this model for professional learning to provide mentor-teachers access to high-quality professional development resources with performance-based demonstrations of mastery. The curriculum from 2014 was repurposed and converted to seven MCs aligned with the topic areas outlined in the section of this paper describing the curriculum.

One advantage of the MC platform is that it provides access to professional learning even when an EPP or state have not developed or implemented the desired resources. The platform also allows for individuals to choose the timing and pace of their professional learning.

Model C—Blended Learning

In our use of MCs at NEA, a challenge was found when micro-credentials are implemented as a means for professional learning without support of a "professional community." Unless educators intentionally choose to collaborate with others who are also studying the same topic, the completion rate is significantly lower than when they *do* collaborate.

For this reason, NEA also repurposed the curriculum for mentor-teacher support to be offered in a blended learning format—face-to-face initial and concluding meetings with virtual meetings of a cohort over an eight-week period. The content was also enhanced so that a first-semester course experience utilized the bulk of the original curriculum, but a second-semester course was added with a focus on practicing conferencing skills, observation skills, and communications skills while working with an actual teacher-candidate or mentoring a peer.

The blended learning model provided the support of a cohort and the opportunity for collaboration. Another feature of the blended learning model is that cohorts or subgroups of participants identify some common concern or problem of implementation during the semester and engage in either the development of a strategy to solve the problem or an action research project to address the concern.

Model D—Emerging Possibilities

A new model for delivery of supports for mentor-teachers was under development at the time of writing this chapter. Louisiana Department of Education (LDoE) was in search of potential program providers for its own mentor-teacher development program with a goal of 2,500 mentor-teachers trained and ready to serve in accordance with state policy working with all new teacher-candidates during yearlong clinical practice placements.

The NEA curriculum became a supplement to a full implementation of the LDoE model utilizing Louisiana Association of Educators (LAE) as the program coordinator and trainer of trainers for future mentors.

RESULTS

Model A—Workshop Implementation

EPP partnerships. Three EPPs explored potential partnerships with NEA affiliates. The first of these worked with its state department of education to implement a pilot to establish a training cadre and is briefly discussed in the section on state department partnerships.

A second EPP seemed to be a natural fit as one of its faculty members helped to develop the NEA resources. The project was presented to their dean, and discussions for implementation were in process when the concerns arose that participating in a project with NEA might be viewed as inequitable for a competing organization on campus. While the competing organization did not offer any supports for mentor-teachers, the EPP decided that using NEA resources could be viewed as an endorsement of one organization over the other.

The third EPP potential project ended before implementation when application for grant funding from an external provider was not approved.

State department partnerships. Growing from the interest of an EPP to establish a partnership, a project with a state department of education was initiated and resulted in a two-day workshop for future trainers of mentor-teachers in June 2016. The participant list for that event included both P–12 educators who would return to their districts to support others as mentor-teachers and EPP faculty from three states who anticipated using the training with their own candidates. While survey data of participants was extremely favorable regarding the appropriate content of the training and effective professional learning methodology, this program was offered only once, and data collection did not continue beyond post-session surveys as the coordinator of the program at the state department of education left for another position. No one at the state department was assigned to continue the program.

State affiliate partnership. Policymakers in Louisiana determined in 2018 that within three years, they would require all mentor-teachers to be trained before they would be eligible to host teacher-candidates. They devised a plan to prepare 2,500 trained mentor-teachers within the three-year time frame. Initially, no curriculum or program specifications were established. The Louisiana Association of Educators (LAE) and its Teaching and Learning Center partnered with NEA to deliver a workshop for potential mentor-teachers in March 2018. While sixteen teachers signed up for the one-day event, twenty-three arrived and participated.

The venue, adequate for twenty, was cramped, but the participants unanimously rated both the relevance and quality of the training as 5/5. Comments on session evaluations confirmed that the content provided worthwhile tools for their role as mentor-teacher. At least three participants were already serving as mentors for alternate-route first-year teachers and commented that they wished they had begun their mentoring experience with the knowledge and skills practiced in this session.

More recent outreach to the 2018 participants generated five responses, again with unanimous affirmation that their experiences helped them to fulfill their mentor-teacher roles. In one instance, the mentor-teacher was in her second year in the classroom and was working with an alternate route first-year teacher from a program that included no clinical practice. For this mentor-teacher, the NEA/LAE training was described as "absolutely essential" for their success.

By the summer of 2018, the Louisiana Department of Education (LDoE) had formalized its training plan. Its new model will be discussed in the "Emerging Possibilities" section.

Model B—Micro-Credentials

The Micro-Credential (MC) "stack" consists of seven MCs aligned with the topic areas described in the Curriculum section of this paper. Participants have enrolled in one or more of the individual MCs, but none have pursued the entire set of seven and data on performance on the discrete MCs is currently too limited for analysis.

Model C—Blended Learning

One of NEA's first Blended Learning pilots of this program occurred during the 2018–2019 school year in Louisiana. Even though a competing state-endorsed training was being piloted, seven participants enrolled in the blended learning experience. In some ways, it most closely aligns with the crucial principles of adult learning providing autonomy for participants to choose a problem of practice and engage in greater levels of study and development of either action research or some authentic project to address the area of concern.

Feedback from participants through questionnaires and interviews surfaced a deep appreciation for the opportunity to support colleagues both within the blended learning training and to support a teacher-candidate in the classroom. At the same time, participants became aware of their own reluctance to let go of the classroom to a teacher-candidate. This spirit of support for each other, even with difficult issues such as "letting go," served as a motivation for one participant to continue to join in collaborative Zoom meetings even after deciding they would not have time to complete all requirements to receive credit. The cohort and learning experience were too powerful to abandon.

Surveys also provided feedback on enhancements for the program. These ideas included focused attention on trauma-informed pedagogy and coming to terms with letting the teacher-candidate "make mistakes" as part of their growth experience.

Model D—Emerging Possibilities

A cadre of nine LAE teacher members were selected in the spring of 2019 to assist with editing and adapting the LDoE pilot curriculum. Based on the revisions and model for delivery proposed, LAE was approved in August 2019 by LDoE to serve as an official provider of the training. To create more manageable demands for the presenters, the cadre of nine was divided into three teams of three, each team to present three days of the nine-day LDoE training.

All nine also will provide support to the entire group of mentors that participate in the training. While only minor changes were made to the LDoE training (available through the LDoE website at http://www.louisianabelieves.com/teaching/louisiana-mentor-teachers) for the course sequence to be conducted from September 2019 to February 2020, the cadre identified two significant gaps they hope to rectify by incorporating elements from the NEA curriculum into LAE's version of the LDoE training in subsequent years.

Those two elements been highly regarded in earlier face-to-face pilots. They are (1) sharing both a research base and simulation activities designed to deepen the understanding of culture and race to support culturally responsive practices for both mentors and teacher-candidates, and (2) helping mentors build strong partnerships and understanding of curriculum and expectations of their mentee's respective EPPs.

DISCUSSION

One of the greatest challenges in offering a high-quality curriculum through varied pathways was finding and sustaining partnerships. In some instances, projects were deemed unfeasible without grant funding. It could be that building some form of financial support into partnership agreements will increase the opportunities for collaboration. In other settings, projects that successfully begin may be short-lived due to changes in personnel within a key partner. Systems are needed to ensure sustainability over time. It may be that partnership agreements should include a mechanism for ongoing staffing support even when personnel changes do occur. And finally, there will inevitably be multiple organizations that can provide clubs, projects, and extended learning opportunities to teacher-candidates. An EPP may greatly limit access to quality resources for teacher-candidates, though, if it only allows programs that all partner organizations can offer.

Feedback from participants in both workshop and blended learning models indicate that the curriculum and experiences are perceived as valuable with practical application for mentoring relationship. It is too early to draw conclusions on limited data available for micro-credentials, but it is anticipated that completion rates will be higher when two or more participants collaborate and support each other while working on the micro-credentials.

CONCLUSIONS

One goal for future use of the resources of the NEA curriculum, regardless of delivery model, would be to develop partnerships that systematically evaluate program content and effective delivery strategies.

A second goal for NEA is to find ways to scale its offering so that experienced teachers who are well-trained for the role of mentor will be readily available at sites that host teacher-candidates across the country, regardless of the policy environment of each state and the varied capacity of EPPs to offer training and support. The NEA continues to build its own capacity to address this crucial need through preparation of additional facilitators for the blended learning model and through its Teacher Leadership Institute (TLI), inviting TLI participants in ten states to embrace cooperating teacher training or early career mentoring as their capstone projects.

NEA's 2017 *Great Teaching and Learning* report offered recommendations beyond suggesting professional development for each career phase. It identified five "keys to transformation," elements of school culture crucial for learning and success of students and educators alike. A third goal for NEA would be that these keys to transformation would guide the design and implementation of any program to support mentor-teachers or teacher-candidates. EPPs and policymakers are encouraged to join NEA in utilizing the vision and recommendations of the 2017 report to guide future programs and partnerships.

REFERENCES

American Association of Colleges for Teacher Education. (2018). *A pivot toward clinical practice, its lexicon, and the renewal of educator preparation: A Report of the AACTE Clinical Practice Commission.* Retrieved from https://secure.aacte.org/apps/rl/res_get.php?fid=3750&ref=rl.

Coleman, J. S., Campbell, E. Q., Hobson, C. J., McPartland, J., Mood, A. M., Weinfeld, F. D., & York, R. L. (1966). *Equality of educational opportunity.* U.S. Department of Health, Education, and Welfare. Retrieved from https://files.eric.ed.gov/fulltext/ED012275.pdf.

Council of Chief State School Officers. (2012). *Our responsibility, our promise: Transforming educator preparation and entry into the profession.* Retrieved from https://ccsso.org/sites/default/files/2017-10/Our%20Responsibility%20Our%20Promise_2012.pdf.

Hall, D. M., Hughes, M. A., & Thelk, A. D. (2017). Developing mentorship skills in clinical faculty: A best practices approach to supporting beginning teachers. *Teacher Educators Journal, 10*(Spring), 77–98.

Henning, J. E., Gut, D. M., & Beam, P. C. (2019). *Building mentoring capacity in teacher education: A guide to clinically-based practice.* New York: Routledge.

Killion, J., & Harrison, C. (2017). *Taking the lead: New roles for teachers and school-based Coaches.* Oxford, OH: Learning Forward.

Knight, J. (2011). What good coaches do. *Educational Leadership, 69*(2), 18–22.

Knight, J. (2018). *The impact cycle: What instructional coaches should do to foster powerful improvements in teaching.* Thousand Oaks, CA: Corwin.

Knowles, M. S. (1973). *The adult learner: A neglected species.* Houston: Gulf Publishing Company.

Lipton, L., & Wellman, B. (2018). *Mentoring matters: A practical guide to learning-focused relationships*. Charlotte, VT: Mira Via.

National Council for Accreditation of Teacher Education. (2010). *Transforming teacher education through clinical practice: A national strategy to prepare effective teachers*. Retrieved from http://caepnet.org/~/media/Files/caep/accreditation-resources/blue-ribbon-panel.pdf.

National Education Association. (2011). *Transforming teaching: Connecting professional responsibility with student learning*. Retrieved from http://www.nea.org/home/49981.htm.

National Education Association. (2017). *Great teaching and learning: Creating the culture to support professional excellence*. Retrieved from https://www.nea.org/assets/docs/Great%20Teaching%20and%20Learning%20Report.pdf.

Osler, J. (2016). *Beyond brochures: Practicing "soul care" in the recruitment of teachers of color*. San Francisco Teacher Residency. Retrieved from: http://www.sfteacherresidency.org/wp-content/uploads/2015/08/SFTR-SoulCare-Final.pdf.

Papay, J. P., & Kraft, M. A. (2017). Developing workplaces where teachers stay, improve, & succeed: Recent evidence on the importance of school climate for teacher success. In E. Quintero, (Ed.). *Teaching in context: How social aspects of school and school systems shape teachers' development and effectiveness* (pp. 15–35). Cambridge, MA: Harvard Education Press.

Patterson, K., Grenny, J., McMillan, R., & Switzler, A. (2012). *Crucial conversations: Tools for talking when stakes are high*. New York: McGraw Hill.

Peters, T., Margolin, M., Fragnoli, K., & Bloom, D. (2016). What's race got to do with it? Preservice teachers and White racial identity. *Current Issues in Education*, 19(1). Retrieved from http://cie.asu.edu/ojs/index.php/cieatasu/article/view/1661.

Pink, D. H. (2009). *Drive: The surprising truth about what motivates us*. New York, NY: Riverhead Books.

Ross, D. L. (2002). Cooperating teachers facilitating reflective practice for student teachers in a professional development school. *Education*, *122*(4), 682–87.

Sayeski, K., & Paulsen, K. (2012). Student teacher evaluations of cooperating teachers as indices of effective mentoring. *Teacher Education Quarterly, 39*(2), 117–30. Retrieved from http://www.jstor.org/stable/23479675.

About the Editors

Dr. Philip E. Bernhardt is a professor of secondary education and associate director of the Honors Program at the Metropolitan State University of Denver. Dr. Bernhardt has spent over two decades working in public schools, including eight years as a secondary social studies teacher. He frequently presents on topics that include barriers to higher education; co-teaching; academic tracking; teacher professional development; curriculum design and assessment; and teacher preparation, induction, and mentoring. Dr. Bernhardt has published numerous journal articles and book chapters, and he co-published *Digital Citizenship: Promoting Wellness for Thriving in a Connected World*, a textbook designed to support middle and high school students' understanding of their digital footprint and the unintended consequences associated with habitual use of the internet and social media. Dr. Bernhardt earned his MAT in social studies education from Boston University, and he received his doctorate in curriculum and instruction from George Washington University.

About the Editors

Dr. Thomas R. Conway is currently chairperson of teacher education and assistant director of the Honors Program at Cabrini University in Radnor, Pennsylvania. Dr. Conway spent nineteen years teaching and administrating at the high school level before moving full-time into higher education. Dr. Conway has worked on several Pennsylvania grants that have researched the use of instructional coaching and mentoring during the student teaching/clinical internship timeframe of teacher preparation. In addition to this grant work, Dr. Conway has also worked on grants that have focused on early intervention strategies and mentoring within the early childhood context. Dr. Conway has presented on mentoring, coaching, and topics in secondary education and early childhood at state, national, and international conferences. Dr. Conway earned his BA in secondary education/social studies, an MA in theological and pastoral studies, and an EdD in educational leadership from Saint Joseph's University.

Dr. Greer M. Richardson is currently the director of graduate programs and associate professor of education at La Salle University in Philadelphia, Pennsylvania. Dr. Richardson is also the associate director of the Philadelphia Regional Noyce Partnership, a collaborative of regional higher education institutions dedicated to supporting the STEM teacher pipeline. In recent years, Dr. Richardson has also led two instructional coaching grant initiatives supporting the development of teacher-leaders as well as early learning school principals. Dr. Richardson has presented extensively on teacher mentoring, new teacher induction, instructional coaching, and collaborative partnerships at state, national, and international conferences. Her most recent co-publication, entitled *Using instructional coaching to support student teacher–cooperating teacher relationships*, highlights the efficacy of instructional coaching to improve the teacher-candidate–mentor-teacher relationships. Dr. Richardson earned her M Ed from Rutgers University and her PhD from Temple University, both in educational psychology.

About the Contributors

Dr. Kristien Zenkov is a professor of education and coordinates the Secondary Education (SEED) program at George Mason University. He is the author and editor of more than 150 articles and book chapters and seven books, focusing on teacher education, literacy pedagogy and curricula, social justice education, and school-university partnerships. Dr. Zenkov is a long-time boundary-spanning educator and regularly conducts project-based clinical experiences with youths and preservice and in-service teachers, while co-directing the "Through Students' Eyes" photovoice project through which young people document with photographs and writings what they believe about citizenship, justice, school, and literacy.

Dr. Audra Parker is a professor and academic program coordinator in elementary education in the School of Education at George Mason University. In addition to teaching courses in elementary methods and management, she partners as a university facilitator at Garfield Elementary, a PDS site. Her research centers on innovations in clinical teacher preparation in elementary education and elementary organizational structures. She has published her research in *The New Educator*, *Action in Teacher Education*, and *School-University Partnerships*, and she serves as a leader in the field of clinical teacher preparation through active engagement in NAPDS (National Association for Professional Development Schools) and ATE (Association in Teacher Education).

Holly Glaser is a PhD candidate in the College of Education and Human Development at George Mason University, where she is pursuing a dual specialization in teaching and teacher education and diversity and equity in gifted education. Prior to beginning her doctoral studies, Holly taught fourth grade general education and fourth grade gifted education in both Virginia and Oregon, as well as served as a gifted resource specialist in a high-poverty school. She was nominated for the Region IV Teacher of the Year award by the Virginia Association for the Gifted in 2015. Holly's research focuses on creating classroom contexts for developing talent in students from culturally and linguistically diverse backgrounds.

Amy Vessel is the James R. Mays Endowed Professor and executive director of the Clinical Residency & Recruitment Center in Louisiana Tech University's College of Education.

Dawn Basinger is the Herbert H. McElveen Endowed Professor and associate dean for academic affairs in the College of Education at Louisiana Tech University.

Amy Rogers is an associate professor and chair of the Education Department at Lycoming College, Williamsport, Pa. She has over twenty-five years' experience in public education as a social studies teacher, literacy coach, and professor of education. Amy holds degrees from Lycoming College, Bloomsburg University, and earned her PhD at The Pennsylvania State University. Amy is active in the education profession with her work as a member of the Association of Teacher Educator (ATE) national task member, board member of the Pennsylvania Association of Colleges and Teacher Educators (PAC-TE), a member of the PA Deans of Education Forum, and a program reviewer for the Pennsylvania Department of Education. She serves as co-chair for Lycoming College's Middle States Accreditation and chief certification and accreditation officer.

Courtney Dexter has worked as a special educator for fifteen years, both in K-12 and higher education capacities. She earned a BA in history from Southern Methodist University, an MEd in secondary education from Texas State University, and MEd in special education from Penn State University, and most recently completed a PhD in special education at Penn State University. From 2015–2020, she held the position of assistant professor of education at Lycoming College, heading up the special education certification program. Her research interests include explicit instruction and behavioral interventions for students with high-incidence disabilities, as well as using video reflection and analysis to build effective teaching behaviors in pre-service teachers. Courtney recently moved back home to Texas to be closer to family, and is excited to return to special education work at the elementary level in the Dallas Independent School district.

John Lando Carter is an assistant professor at Middle Tennessee State University and a former high school English teacher. He teaches in the MTSU Residency I program as well as the MTSU ALSI doctoral program.

Josh Tipton is an assistant professor and EdD program director at Lincoln Memorial University. He is a former middle and high school teacher, administrator, and district supervisor.

Ashlee Hover is an assistant professor at Middle Tennessee State University and a former elementary school teacher. She teaches in the MTSU Residency I program and serves as the coordinator for the Curriculum and Instruction Master's degree at MTSU.

Maureen P. Hall is a full professor of education at the University of Massachusetts Dartmouth. As a teacher-educator, she focuses on the intersections between and among mindfulness, literacies, and social emotional learning (SEL) to improve instruction. She has published more than twenty articles in peer-reviewed journals, and her books include *Transforming Literacy: Changing Lives through Reading and Writing* (Emerald Publishing, 2011) with Robert Waxler, and, in 2019, *The Whole Person: Embodying Teaching and Learning through Lectio and Visio Divina* (Rowman & Littlefield) with Jane Dalton and Catherine Hoyser.

Christopher Clinton is a full-time lecturer, graduate program director, and co-chair of the STEM Education and Teacher Development Department at the University of Massachusetts Dartmouth. As a teacher-educator, he focuses on teacher candidate "readiness" and developing sustainable relationships with K-12 stakeholders. He has been the founding educator/administrator of an Urban Pilot School, the first Charter School in Massachusetts and an Urban Innovations Academy. His consultancy with NIET and DESE resulted in the Massachusetts *Candidate Assessment of Performance (CAP)* in 2016. His research interests are in integrating stakeholders in teacher preparation, mentoring, teacher leadership and Charter/Innovation school startup.

Lorena Claeys is the director of clinical professional experiences at the Academy for Teacher Excellence Research Center. Her research focuses on Latino teacher preparation and retention.

Claudia Treviño García is an assistant professor in practice in the Residency 2.0 Program at the University of Texas at San Antonio. Her research focuses on teacher cultural efficacy development, bilingual/biliteracy education programs, teacher recruitment, and retention.

Belinda Bustos Flores is a professor of bicultural-bilingual studies and associate dean of professional preparation and partnerships at the University of Texas at San Antonio. Her research focuses on teacher recruitment, development, preparation, and retention.

Lucinda M. Juárez is an assistant professor of education at Our Lady of the Lake University in San Antonio. Her research focuses on critical literacy instruction, science of teaching reading (STR), writing instruction, technology infusion in instruction, virtual learning, cultural efficacy development, bilingual/biliteracy instruction, and clinical and teacher literacy coaching.

Lisa Santillán is an assistant professor in practice in the Residency 2.0 Program at the University of Texas at San Antonio. Her primary research includes: bilingual education, biliteracy/biculturalism, second language learners, teacher identity, teacher pedagogy and preparation, culturally-efficacious teaching/development, qualitative approaches to research and sociocultural theory.

Lucinda N. Sohn is an assistant professor in practice at the University of Texas at San Antonio. She has been a field experience instructor, clinical site supervisor, secondary science teacher, and facilitator of environmental education programs.

Jennifer Gilardi Swoyer is an assistant professor in practice at the University of Texas at San Antonio. Her research focuses on teacher identify formation, mentoring through coaching, differentiated instruction for emergent bilinguals, and teacher recruitment and retention.

Timothy Lintner is Carolina Trustee Professor of Education at the University of South Carolina Aiken. He presently serves as the secondary social studies program coordinator and director of the Teaching Fellows program. His current research examines collaborative partnerships and practices between social studies and special education.

About the Contributors

Bridget Coleman is professor of education at the University of South Carolina Aiken. She teaches mathematics methods courses and supervises field experiences. She has actively worked with PDS partners for over a decade and serves as a PDS university liaison

Jeremy Rinder is instructor of curriculum and instruction at the University of South Carolina Aiken. He teaches multiple courses including science and social studies methods for early childhood education, social studies methods for elementary education, and classroom management. All of the courses he teaches are housed in Professional Development Schools within the local school district.

Deborah McMurtrie is associate professor of education at the University of South Carolina Aiken. She is the middle level education program coordinator and chair of the Professional Development Schools (PDS) committee. Her research interests include interdisciplinary curriculum development and culturally responsive practice in teacher preparation programs.

Rachelle Curcio is a clinical assistant professor in elementary education at the University of South Carolina. Dr. Curcio's research is grounded in an inquiry stance and focuses on various structures of clinically-centered teacher preparation for twenty-first century contexts. Specifically, she has expertise in supervision and coaching, pedagogy for embedded teacher preparation, and professional development school partnerships. Currently, Dr. Curcio works within several initial certification programs aimed at providing unique pathways into teaching within the state of South Carolina.

Alyson Adams is clinical associate professor and associate director for teaching and teacher education in the School of Teaching and Learning in the University of Florida's College of Education. She works with several graduate programs for full-time working professionals focused on social-justice and advocacy in education. Dr. Adams has expertise in teacher education, supervision and coaching, online course design and development, and adult learning. Current work includes a focus on the education doctorate and support for educators moving to remote/online instruction.

Sheri C. Hardee is the dean and a professor in the College of Education at the University of North Georgia. She has a PhD in social foundations in education from the University of South Carolina. She utilizes postcolonial and feminist intersectionality frameworks to examine equity and equality in regard to access to and support in institutions of higher education, starting with support provided within middle and high school environments. In particular, she has examined both mentoring and college-ready support programs. She has taught both undergraduate and graduate courses in the social foundations of education and has published articles in *Teaching Education*, *The Journal of Educational Foundations*, and *Thresholds in Education*.

Lauren C. Johnson is the assistant dean and an associate professor in the College of Education at the University of North Georgia. A graduate of Columbia College and Teachers College of Columbia University, she received her PhD in applied anthropology from the University of South Florida. Dr. Johnson has taught at the K-12 and university levels in the United States and abroad. She has conducted research in the areas of cultural studies, applied anthropology, and the anthropology of education on issues of race and inequality, gender and sexuality, immigration, and diversity pedagogy. She has published peer-reviewed articles and presented at numerous academic conferences on the topics of diversity in teacher education, social justice education, ethnographic research, and socioeconomic inequality in the Caribbean region. Her most recent project is "Teaching Social Justice in Racially Divided Contexts," a grant-funded study that explores trends and challenges for teacher education programs in post-Apartheid South Africa.

Blake West was a P-12 mathematics and computer science teacher for thirty-seven years. During this career he also developed a new-teacher induction program in his school district and piloted the role of peer assistant in his school. He helped establish a statewide Teacher Leadership Academy and served as chair of the Kansas Learning First Alliance from 2007–2009. In 2015, Dr. West left his classroom to join the Teacher Quality Department at NEA's Center for Great Public Schools. At NEA, Blake's responsibilities include a major focus on teacher preparation and supporting mentor teachers for Aspiring Educators.

www.ingramcontent.com/pod-product-compliance
Lightning Source LLC
Chambersburg PA
CBHW030140240426
43672CB00005B/206